politics@media

David D. Perlmutter, Editor

MONEY
POWER&

Published in cooperation with the

Kevin P. Reilly Center for Media and Public Affairs

 Louisiana State University Press   *Baton Rouge*

ELECTIONS

HOW CAMPAIGN FINANCE REFORM
SUBVERTS AMERICAN DEMOCRACY

RODNEY A. SMITH

Published by Louisiana State University Press
Copyright © 2006 by Rodney A. Smith
All rights reserved
Manufactured in the United States of America
First printing

Designer: Barbara Neely Bourgoyne
Typeface: Berthold Baskerville Book
Printer and binder: Edwards Brothers, Inc.

Library of Congress Cataloging-in-Publication Data
Smith, Rodney A., 1941–
  Money, power, and elections : how campaign finance reform subverts American democracy /
Rodney A. Smith.
        p. cm. – (Politics@media)
  Includes bibliographical references.
  ISBN 0-8071-3128-8 (cloth : alk. paper)
  1. Campaign funds–United States. 2. Democracy–United States. I. Title. II. Series.
JK1991.S58 2006
324.7'80973–dc22
                                                                    2005023906

To my wife
Mary Margaret

and

my four children
Kelli, Nani, Rhett, and Parker

For making it all worthwhile.

CONTENTS

TABLES

FIGURES

ACKNOWLEDGMENTS

Because the interaction of money and politics is such a complex and often misunderstood process, writing this book with clarity and precision was difficult. Any and all comments, interpretations, and errors of fact contained within this book are entirely my own. Whatever inaccuracies and weaknesses this book may contain would have been far worse without the kind help of friends.

First and foremost, I want to thank Dr. David Perlmutter, associate professor at Louisiana State University, whose intellectual and conceptual contributions were invaluable, as was his editor's eye. Dr. Thomas H. Landess, who taught in the Politics and Literature Program at the University of Dallas, was my main sounding board for the ideas and content of the book. Tom's researching genius and his daughter Kate's Internet research skills were extremely helpful in the development of the major concepts. The wise counsel and insights of Brian Kraft and Kristi Negri, helped transform my manuscript into a far better book. Mark Braden, an expert in federal election law, endeavored to keep my text accurate with regard to legal matters. Others who added immensely to improving the quality of the book include Bob Packwood, Tom Edmonds, Raymond Strother, Jim Lavin, Donna Anderson, Robin Breckenridge, Joshua Lewis, Jodi Bannerman, Oscar W. Cranz Jr., and my wife, Mary Margaret. To each I want to say thank you.

I want to thank Dr. Clyde Wilcox, professor of government at Georgetown University, for validating the accuracy of the database that is the backbone of the book. I owe a large debt of gratitude to the combined efforts of the many people who treated the creation of the database as if it were their own, including Scott, Stacey, Zack, Gene, Josh, Katie, Nani, John, and the small army of temps who spent countless hours checking the correctness of more than two gigabytes of information.

Finally, I want to offer particular thanks to Louisiana State University, the Reilly Center for Media and Public Affairs at LSU, LSU Press, and their respective staffs for investing in this project and approving its publication.

RODNEY A. SMITH
Washington, DC
2005

MONEY, POWER, AND ELECTIONS

1 THE FOLLY OF REFORM

To err is natural; to rectify error is glory.

George Washington

As I recall it, Thursday, April 6, 1972, was a picture-perfect spring day in Washington, DC. The cherry blossoms had just lost their dazzling brilliance, the many flower gardens scattered throughout the city were beginning to stir, and the air was fresh and mild. It was a wonderful moment to be alive and living in our nation's capital.

Unaware of the beauty of the day, a small, dedicated group of staffers in a downtown office were frantically working on an emergency project behind locked doors that absolutely, without fail, had to be finished prior to midnight.

The office was located at 1701 Pennsylvania Avenue, NW, catercorner to the White House. In 1972, Financial General Bankshares, Inc., owned the building. The company was a bank and insurance conglomerate controlled by General George Olmstead. At that time Olmstead was an internationally known financier with considerable political clout who was particularly proud of his brief army career serving as a brigadier general during the Second World War.

Once I had the good fortune to stand briefly on Olmstead's twelfth floor office balcony and gaze directly down on the White House. It is the only office in the city with this commanding view. Standing there I was suddenly seized by a tingling sense of "Potomac Fever"—also known as the lust for power. This brief encounter gave me a glimpse at what drives politics and politicians. It's a moment I've never forgotten.

Oblivious to the grandeur of the view nine floors above, the clerks on the third floor were busy sorting and counting stacks of cash. There were some checks. But most of the money was raw cash, and lots of it. It was their charge to get several million dollars deposited in Olmstead's bank located on the first floor before midnight. To help accomplish this task, the bank had agreed to stay open late.

Much of the money was neatly lined up in columns on the floor, reminiscent of military formations. Other stacks of cash were piled on tables. Once the record keeping had been completed, a deposit slip was filled out and double-checked. Periodically, a clerk or two would slip down the back stairs with several bags full of deposits. The bank had set up a separate room to help expedite the depositing process.

Just before midnight, the last deposit was made. The clerical staff had met their deadline. At midnight a new law would take effect making it illegal to add further undisclosed deposits into this secret account. The clerical staff and their boss, Maurice Stans, were elated that they had beaten the clock. Stans was then the finance chairman of the Committee to Re-Elect the President (CREEP) and, prior to resigning in December 1971, had been secretary of commerce under President Richard Nixon. Tragically, their success that day in filling the coffers of a clandestine bank account helped set the stage for funding a series of illicit acts that would forever alter the nature of American politics.

The next morning, Friday, April 7, 1972, at 12:01 A.M., the Federal Election Campaign Act (FECA) of 1971 officially became law. Among other things, FECA, for the first time in American history, required the meaningful reporting of campaign contributions and expenditures by political organizations and candidate committees. While it was by no means a perfect law, FECA was a significant step in the right direction. It enabled the American public to better understand how political campaigns and organizations were funded. If they so desired, citizens could use this new information to adjust their voting behavior.

It had taken America nearly two hundred years to come to grips with the fact that full disclosure of political contributions and expenditures was important. The electorate has the right—and the need—to know how campaigns and political committees are funded and by whom.

Full disclosure of information, including amounts given, names, addresses, and other such relevant information about political donors and vendors, is consistent with the intent of the Framers of the Constitution and the principles imbedded in it. Yet for most of our country's history, such information had seldom, if ever, been available in any meaningful way. The passage of FECA was an important step toward correcting this deficiency.

Had Nixon's reelection campaign in 1972 honorably and openly complied with the spirit and intent of this new law, the Watergate tragedy might never have happened. If CREEP had reported the more than $20 million in contributions it had collected prior to April 6, it would have been obligated it to report any expenditure from those funds. Given this level of public disclosure, no one at CREEP would have given a free-wheeling character like G. Gordon Liddy, or anyone else, signature control over a separate, segregated bank account.

The people running CREEP may not have been overly endowed with moral sensitivities, but they had plenty of political savvy. With the press looking over their shoulder as a result of these newly required public disclosure reports, there is simply no way they would have allowed anyone to have autonomous control over a large sum of money. Additionally, the internal control systems that are inherently necessary to run a fully disclosed financial operation effectively would have provided CREEP a reasonably efficient safeguard against illegal expenditures of the type involved in the Watergate scandal. CREEP, unfortunately, chose a different approach.

On Saturday, June 17, 1972, a little over two months after the last slush fund deposit was made, five men were arrested at the Watergate complex at 600 New Hampshire Avenue NW. Initially, this break-in seemed like a petty burglary hardly deserving of media coverage. However, there was an odd twist that made the story particularly interesting. One of the people taken to jail that day was a man by the name of James McCord, who happened to be the security director for CREEP. He was also a close associate of G. Gordon Liddy, another security consultant retained by CREEP. The fuse had been lit. A chain reaction of events had begun. The whole sordid mess would eventually ignite the biggest and most famous political scandal in American history.

In retrospect, the Watergate fiasco proved that the Founders' constitutional handiwork was fundamentally sound. A president was forced to resign. Months earlier a vice president had also been forced to resign because of criminal behavior committed when he had served as governor of Maryland. Before the Watergate debacle ended, more than forty government officials would be indicted, and some would serve time in jail. The constitutional system of checks and balances, the freedom of the press, and, ultimately, citizen sovereignty along with full disclosure of financial records proved stronger than the dishonesty of a few power-hungry officials, no matter how highly placed. Democracy, as defined by our Constitution, prevailed.

Had the saga of Watergate ended there, the whole episode might have strengthened confidence in America's unique system of government. Unfortunately that is not what happened. Instead, Watergate gave birth to a new sense of suspicion and distrust. Seemingly overnight, our country's confidence in the political processes devised by the constitutional Framers was undermined as never before.

More than thirty years later, the negative impact of Watergate on our competitive election process is now unmistakable. Tragically, the slush fund created by CREEP prior to April 6, 1972, the criminal break-in that that secret bank account funded, the massive coverup orchestrated by the president himself, and the unprecedented and prolonged media and press barrage all fused together to create an emotionally charged animosity toward money in politics. Over time it has evolved into paranoia.

Indeed, this negative mind-set has gained considerable strength nationwide and has created a frenzy for campaign finance reform. In reaction to Watergate, Congress passed the Federal Election Campaign Act of 1974, which imposed contribution limits on all political entities.[1]

But other, more recent controversies have also added fuel to the fires for reform. For example, the fund-raising improprieties in the Clinton administration in the mid-1990s, including the acceptance of foreign contributions that had long been illegal, again put the issue of campaign finance reform on the front page of every newspaper in the country. But it was the sleaziness of the Enron debacle and its management's perceived (not proven) attempts to buy government favors with campaign contributions that finally forced the passage of the Bipartisan Campaign Reform Act of 2002 (BCRA). Most Americans believe this innocent-sounding act of Congress and related Supreme Court decisions to be little more than benevolent tinkering with our election process—the closing of a few "loopholes." However, the sobering truth is that these actions have revolutionary consequences that adversely affect every American.[2]

In the months before BCRA passed, the *Gallup Poll Monthly* reported that among people who said they were following the Enron story closely, 80 percent believed new campaign finance laws were necessary, compared with just 55 percent who were not following the story closely.[3] The resulting laws that Congress passed in the emotional aftermath of these watershed events and the subsequent court decisions handed down have altered the foundation of American democracy.

In addition, this obsession with reform has spawned a cottage industry of elected officials, lawyers, academics, political activists, media personalities, and columnists dedicated to purging the American political process of money. It is as if money itself were somehow the root of all political evil.

Among the newspapers with the ten highest circulations in America, eight largely espoused proreform views. Only one, the *Wall Street Journal,* consistently opposed the type of campaign finance reform that has become the law of the land.

Unfortunately, many of these well-intentioned reformers in the press, in Congress, and elsewhere have rushed to support campaign finance reform without first carefully and scrupulously considering any of its unintended consequences. In their zeal to correct a *perceived* problem, they have unwittingly created a new inequality, which, left unchecked, threatens to destroy our competitive election process and ultimately our survival as a free people.

Physics says that a thing set in motion stays in motion until something stops it. In physics that "something" might be friction or gravity; in history, a misguided notion might be brought to rest by truth. I hope this book provides that truth. My purpose in writing is to call attention to the destructive consequences of campaign finance reform, and I hope it helps initiate a counterforce that puts an end to those consequences. Specifically to be addressed is what I believe is now undeniable fact: however noble their goal, these campaign finance laws and court decisions have imposed a monetary straightjacket that is literally shutting down our competitive two-party election process.

For most of my adult life I have been a political fund-raiser, a vocation that is regarded by many as slightly less respectable than pool hall hustler, cardsharp, or tax collector. Further, I was part of CREEP back in 1972. Since that time, I have raised hundreds of millions of dollars for political party committees and candidates. Despite the perception of some, I believe that what I do is essential to the survival of American democracy.

In an age dominated by mass media, money buys speech, the kind specifically protected by the First Amendment to the United States Constitution. When candidates lack the money to buy space and time in the media, they are politically paralyzed. Silent, unable to speak, they and their invisible campaigns are totally at the mercy of journalists who may or may not choose to covey their message fairly.

Anyone or anything that deprives candidates of the means to carry their message to the electorate abridges their freedom of speech. And that is precisely what I think so-called campaign finance reform is doing. I firmly believe that when Americans know the facts and understand their implications, they will agree.

When the Founding Fathers set about constructing our democracy, they knew that they were creating a system of government that had to have both the safeguards and the vision to make it applicable to a future they could not begin to imagine. They mined their knowledge of history and philosophy for precedent and guidance, but in some ways it was their understanding of human nature that inspired much of the architecture of the new government. In addition to their idealism, their intellects, and their leadership ability, the Founders had one other important quality. They were realists. They knew about men and their lust for power. They knew about the messiness and the dark side of politics. They knew that two viewpoints could be held in violent opposition while both sides fought with the best intentions for the public good.

While the Founders could never have envisioned the technological advances of our modern world, they would probably not have been at all surprised by what transpires politically in our country. The games of modern-day politics are probably not too different from the compromises and deal-making that occurred in their time. Campaigns could be just as ugly, and information just as distorted, in their time as in ours. But something else is also the same. Many, perhaps even the vast majority, of our elected leaders are in office because they have deeply held beliefs about what is good for our society. They want to have a positive impact on our world. They are interested in the public good. While their lust for power is very real, it is often driven by the desire to have the power to implement an agenda based on ideals.

It is in this no-man's-land between the idealism of leadership and the reality of politics where we get confused and disoriented. We want leaders we look up to, admire, and respect. Yet to gain and hold office, our elected officials must be agile, slick, and shrewd enough to navigate the shark-infested electoral waters of cutthroat politics successfully.

It is out of this clash of idealism and reality that campaign finance reform originates. We want to see our government and our political campaigns run in a gentlemanly (or ladylike) fashion. We want to elect people based on their merits and viewpoints without having to wade through negative campaign ads that may or may not be distortions. We want politics, and especially campaigns, to be polite and courteous.

It isn't going to happen.

As I explain in a later chapter, elections have evolved as an alternative to armed force and war—ballots instead of bullets. And warfare is anything but polite or considerate. It is a tough, vicious conflict in which the stakes are very high. So, too, are the stakes in elections. There is no consolation prize for the runners-up. You win or you lose. And unlike a sporting event, a loss in a campaign can have a profound effect not only on the candidate but on the nation and, in some cases, even on the world. Where ideals and vision and the public good are at stake, people seeking power are going to play to win. Period.

So what did the Founders have to say about elections and campaigns? As we'll see in the chapters that follow, they had quite a bit to say, and they wouldn't be at all happy with the present highly restrictive campaign finance laws.

But this book isn't just about federal campaigns, federal elections, and money. It is about something much more fundamental. It is about our sovereignty. It is about who is going to hold the reins of power. The Founders designed a system to ensure that "the People" would be sovereign—the ultimate authority. Citizen sovereignty is the foundation and the very guarantor of our liberty. It is the cornerstone of our Constitution. If we lose our citizen sovereignty, we have lost our democracy. And that is exactly what is happening.

Through a series of campaign reform laws and Supreme Court decisions, which in combination fly in the face of the intent and language of the Founders' constitutional guarantees, we are on the brink of an age in which only members of a small, highly select group of wealthy individuals and incumbents can successfully run for office. Once there, they are virtually guaranteed to stay in office for life if they choose.

I don't think any Americans, especially the reformers, would desire to have a small, privileged ruling class in America, yet as the data that follow indisputably show, we are practically there. No American would want our ability to oust a politician from office to be hampered. If incumbents cannot, except in extreme cases, be unseated, where is their accountability? What is there to keep them from becoming intoxicated with power? Isn't political invincibility a breeding ground for corruption? Again, as the data show, this is becoming our reality.

By limiting the fund-raising ability of nonwealthy candidates while ignoring the inherent advantages of incumbency and personal wealth, campaign finance reform has created two distinctly different political classes. In one class there are those who have access to personal wealth or a privileged status that enables them to soak up most of the legally available dollars. Everyone else wanting to run for public office is relegated to an inferior political class to which campaign finance reform has reduced the flow of money to a mere trickle. When candidates lack the financial resources to communicate with voters, they are speechless. This is why campaign finance reform has abridged the freedom of speech of *most* candidates—particularly nonwealthy challengers.

Unfortunately, the history of modern campaign finance reform is full of the best intentions, which stem from the idea—perpetuated by the media since Watergate—that money in politics is inherently wicked. I propose that it is not the corruption of money that should be our biggest fear; it is the corruption of power. The problem is that in order to gain real political power, one must first have money. How do we create an acceptable equilibrium between the two? What are the checks and balances? The Founding Fathers embedded in our Constitution an answer to these questions. Their answers worked for some two hundred years. Campaign finance reform has negated those answers. This book explores the nuances of this tragedy.

I have tried to write about what I know—not about what I think. In offering what I hope is a cohesive analysis of the political processes envisioned by the Framers of the Constitution, I wish to hold up for examination how far we have strayed from their original intent. To accomplish this, I have utilized all the resources available to me, including my graduate education in business, my training as a certified public accountant, my more than thirty years of political fund-raising experience, and my lifelong love of history.

In an effort to substantiate and support my observations, I have included a voluminous amount of facts and figures. To give you an advance idea of what I'm up to, I have included Tables 1.1 through 1.4 in this introductory chapter. They summarize the data that support my thesis. Specifically and simply, they show that campaign finance reform is destroying the fundamental fabric of American democracy by making it harder, if not impossible, for nonwealthy candidates to defeat incumbents or opponents with personal wealth.

Table 1.1. Victories by House incumbents and challengers in pre-Buckley, post-Buckley, and post-BCRA eras (general elections only)

	Incumbents	Challengers	Total
PRE-BUCKLEY (1920–1974)			
Election winners	9,733	1,005	10,738
Winning percentage	90.6%	9.4%	100%
Avg. no. of winners per election cycle[a]	348	36	384
POST-BUCKLEY (1976–2000)			
Election winners	4,826	218	5,044
Winning percentage	95.7%	4.3%	100%
Avg. no. of winners per election cycle[a]	371	17	388
Increase (decrease) from pre-Buckley in average no. of winners per election cycle	23	(19)	
Increase (decrease) from pre-Buckley in winning percentage (%)	6.6%	(52.8%)	
POST-BCRA (projected)			
Projected increase (decrease) from post-Buckley in avg. winners per election cycle	8	(8)	
Projected winners per election cycle[a]	379	9	388
Projected winning percentage	97.7%	2.3%	100%
Projected increase (decrease) from pre-Buckley in avg. winners per election cycle	31	(27)	
Projected increase (decrease) from pre-Buckley in avg. winners per election cycle (%)	8.9%	(75%)	

Source: Historical figures compiled from data provided by the Clerk of the House. Post-BCRA projections assume the rate of change to be one-third of that which actually occurred from 1976 to 2000.

[a]Rounded to nearest integer.

The database used to create Tables 1.1 through 1.4 was compiled from information on file with the Clerk of the House in Washington, DC. In reviewing these tables, it is important to note the following:

- The Supreme Court's *Buckley v. Valeo* decision, which drastically changed the financial dynamics of American politics, became effective in January 1976. BCRA, which further restricted the financial aspect of American politics became effective in November 2002. This court decision and this law have created three distinct time periods that can be measured and compared: pre-Buckley (1920–1974), post-Buckley (1976–2002),[4] and post-BCRA (2003 and beyond).

Table 1.2. Margin of victory in House general elections in pre-Buckley, post-Buckley, and post-BCRA eras

	MARGIN OF VICTORY				
	≥15%	10%–14.99%	5%–9.99%	2.5%–4.99%	≤2.49%
PRE-BUCKLEY (1920–1974)					
No. of elections	8,419	1,227	1,258	666	613
Percent	69.1%	10.1%	10.3%	5.5%	5.0%
Avg. per election cycle[a]	301	44	45	24	22
POST-BUCKLEY (1976–2000)					
No. of elections	4,457	394	400	207	197
Percent	78.8%	7.0%	7.1%	3.7%	3.5%
Avg. per election cycle[a]	343	30	31	16	15
Increase (decrease) from pre-Buckley in avg. per election cycle	42	(14)	(14)	(8)	(7)
Increase (decrease) from pre-Buckley in avg. per election cycle (%)	14.0%	(31.8%)	(31.1%)	(33.3%)	(31.8%)
POST-BCRA (projected)					
Projected increase (decrease) from post-Buckley in avg. no. per election cycle	48	–	–	–	(5)
Projected avg. no. per election cycle[a]	≥391	–	–	–	≤10
Projected increase (decrease) from pre-Buckley in avg. no. per election cycle	≥90	–	–	–	(12)
Projected increase (decrease) from pre-Buckley in avg. no. per election cycle (%)	≥30%	–	–	–	(≥55%)

Source: Historical figures compiled from data provided by the Clerk of the House. Post-BCRA projections assume the same rate of change as actually occurred from 1976 to 2000.

[a]Rounded to nearest integer.

- During the modern political era (since 1920), incumbent congressmen and incumbent senators have never been easy to defeat. For the period 1920–1974, the reelection rate of congressmen was 90.6 percent and of senators, 73.8 percent.[5]

- During the post-Buckley era the election rate of House challengers (candidates running against incumbents) has decreased by 52.8

Table 1.3. Victories by Senate incumbents and challengers in pre-Buckley, post-Buckley, and post-BCRA eras (general and special elections, excluding the South)

	Incumbents	Challengers	Total
PRE-BUCKLEY (1920–1974)			
Election winners	454	161	615
Winning percentage	73.8%	26.2%	100%
Avg. no. of winners per election cycle[a]	16	6	22
POST-BUCKLEY (1976–2000)			
Election winners	230	45	275
Winning percentage	83.6%	16.4%	100%
Avg. no. of winners per election cycle[a]	18	3	21
Increase (decrease) from pre-Buckley in avg. no. of winners per election cycle	2	(3)	
Increase (decrease) from pre-Buckley in avg. no of winners (%)	12.5%	(50%)	
POST-BCRA (projected)			
Projected increase (decrease) from post-Buckley in avg. winners per election cycle	1	(1)	
Projected winners per election cycle[a]	19	2	21
Projected winning percentage	90%	10%	100%
Projected increase (decrease) from pre-Buckley in avg. no. of winners per election cycle	3	(4)	
Projected increase (decrease) from pre-Buckley in avg. no. of winners per election cycle (%)	18.8%	(66.7%)	

Source: Historical figures compiled from data provided by the Clerk of the House. Post-BCRA projections assume the rate of change to be one-third of that which actually occurred from 1976 to 2000.

[a]Rounded to nearest integer.

percent, and the rate for Senate challengers winning has decreased by 50 percent.

- During the post-Buckley era, the number of extremely close House races (victory margins of 2.5 percent or less) has decreased by 31.8 percent, and for Senate races it has decreased by 33.3 percent. Shortage of money has been the primary reason losing opponents have been unable to mount competitive campaigns.

- During the post-Buckley era the number of "no-contest" House races (with victory margins of 15 percent or more) has increased by 14 percent, and for the Senate the number has increased by 25 percent.

Table 1.4. Margin of victory in Senate races in pre-Buckley, post-Buckley, and post-BCRA eras (general and special elections, excluding the South)

	MARGIN OF VICTORY				
	≥15%	10%–14.99%	5%–9.99%	2.5%–4.99%	≤2.49%
PRE-BUCKLEY (1920–1974)					
No. of elections	332	120	163	98	90
Percent	41.3%	14.9%	20.3%	12.2%	11.2%
Avg. per election cycle[a]	12	4	6	4	3
POST-BUCKLEY (1976–2000)					
No. of elections	191	45	48	34	32
Percent	54.6%	12.9%	13.7%	9.7%	9.1%
Avg. per election cycle[a]	15	3	4	3	2
Increase (decrease) from pre-Buckley in avg. per election cycle	3	(1)	(2)	(1)	(1)
Increase (decrease) from pre-Buckley in avg. per election cycle (%)	25%	(25%)	(66.7%)	(25%)	(33.3%)
POST-BCRA (projected)					
Projected increase (decrease) from post-Buckley in avg. no. per election cycle	3	–	–	–	(1)
Avg. per election cycle[a]	≥18	–	–	–	≤1
Increase (decrease) from pre-Buckley in avg. no per election cycle	6	–	–	–	(2)
Increase (decrease) from pre-Buckley in avg. no. per election cycle (%)	≥50%	–	–	–	(≥66.7%)

Source: Historical figures compiled from data provided by the Clerk of the House. Post-BCRA projections assume the same rate of change as actually occurred from 1976 to 2000.

[a]Rounded to nearest integer.

- If the trends actually experienced during the post-Buckley era are projected into the post-BCRA era beginning with the 2004 elections, we can expect to see a 75 percent decrease in the numbers of challengers elected to the House, a 66.7 percent decrease in the number of challengers elected to the Senate, a 55 percent decline in the number of extremely close races in the House, a 66.7 percent decline in the number of extremely close races in the Senate, a 30 percent increase in the number of no-contest races in the House, and a 50 percent increase in the number of no-contest races in the Senate. If these trends hold true, congressional incumbency will soon be more an appointment for life than an election to office.

The statistical information in Tables 1.1 through 1.4 should set off alarms for any American who values our right to fair and competitive elections, the right of free exchange of ideas, and our cherished tradition of vigorous public debate. Worse yet, as this book will show in detail, incumbency and personal wealth are now what matter most in winning election to the House and Senate. Money may not buy happiness, but it sure comes in handy when trying to gain a seat in Congress. Without money, there is no freedom of speech.

If we allow campaign finance reform to remain in force, thereby stacking the odds in favor of incumbents and the rich, one essential question lies before us: Is the United States still a democratic republic? Or have we evolved into a plutocracy, an oligarchy pretending to be a republic, or something worse?

While some within the campaign reform movement may choose to ignore the information contained here, neither they nor our country can escape the consequences to which these facts point. If the charge should be made that the data presented are not important, then by implication, the claimant would be saying that the people affected are not important either. Because the people in question are the citizens of America, I would reject such a claim.

Human beings are free to adopt self-destructive ideas and pass self-destructive laws, but they are not free to make either work in a positive way. History is littered with examples of societies that paid a terrible price because they did not realize, or chose to ignore, the consequences of their follies.

Our great folly today is the stubborn and ill-conceived belief that government can control the flow of money into election campaigns without also substantially affecting the outcome of elections. Allowing government interference to dictate winners and losers is not only undemocratic but dangerous, which is why I felt compelled to write this book and why I sincerely hope you will read these pages with an open and inquiring mind.

As we shall see in Chapter 11, full and timely financial disclosure is a better alternative than arbitrary contribution limits. Full disclosure does not undermine the foundation of our unique form of democracy. To remain healthy, our two-party political process demands that there be enough money available for the candidates on both sides to have their message heard. "Enough money" is the threshold. Below this threshold an election can be manipulated by money. Above this threshold money fully disclosed cannot corrupt an election.

2 THE RISE AND FALL OF CITIZEN SOVEREIGNTY

> You are to be hanged by the neck but not until you are dead; for while you are still living your bodies are to be taken down your bowels torn out and burned before your faces; your heads then cut off; your bodies divided into four quarters to be then at the Kings disposal. And may the almighty God have mercy on your souls.
>
> King George III, 1776

When the Founding Fathers signed the Declaration of Independence, they understood that if they failed, they were signing their own death warrants—as King George had proclaimed. Today, when we see these great men memorialized in cold, remote, and lifeless statues, we often dismiss what they risked, endured, and accomplished as no longer relevant to a vastly changed contemporary society. We assume that the issues we confront today are quite different from the ones they faced back in 1776.

If, as a people, we have come to accept such a view of the past, it is because we fail to fully understand the fundamental political principle that lay at the heart of the Founders' willingness to risk death and disgrace. We attempt to pinpoint that principle by calling it "freedom" or "liberty," but these words denote a state of being rather than a political principle. To be sure, the Founders valued "liberty" as a state of being above all others, but they understood that the extent to which freedom is attainable depends on who rules the nation—who is "sovereign."

Most of the Founders had lived their entire adult lives under the sovereignty of George III, which meant that whatever freedom they had enjoyed, he had given to them. And when he so desired, he could take that freedom away. In fact, the greater part of the Declaration of Independence is devoted to the many ways in which the king had deprived the colonies of their freedom. But the part we remember most is what Thomas Jefferson said about the nature of government and sovereignty: governments are instituted to secure "Life, Liberty and the pursuit of Happiness," and that they derive "their just powers from the consent of the governed."

So when the Founders wrote the Declaration of Independence, they weren't merely announcing their departure from the British Empire. They were also propounding a new form of government and, more importantly, a new view of sovereignty. Henceforth, the governed were themselves to be sovereign over themselves rather than cede that power to a king. This radical idea that the ultimate authority of government would rest with the people is what makes the events surrounding, and including, the American Revolution of such historic and worldwide significance.

To the Founding Fathers, "citizen sovereignty"—that is, the unalienable right of citizens to govern themselves, free from the interference of some oppressive authority—wasn't merely an abstraction or an attractive idea to display in a rhetorical document. They had learned its value from personal experience. It was from that experience and their broad understanding of philosophy and history that they forged a new form of government, one based on principles they held dearly—so deeply, in fact, they were willing to risk their lives and property to defend them.

As the "Spirit of 1776" and the memory of the framing of the Constitution continues to recede into our past, we must ask ourselves: Do our love of freedom and respect for the principles embedded in our Constitution that burned so brightly in the latter part of the eighteenth century have any flicker of light left today?

Tragically, at the beginning of the twenty-first century, Americans seem alarmingly indifferent, if not oblivious, to the fact that the precious privilege of citizen sovereignty that the Founders sacrificed so much to acquire is steadily disappearing. This extinction of citizen sovereignty is being caused by unilateral governmental actions that so far have met with little citizen resistance or protest.

In fact, most public opinion polls since the late 1930s show that Americans, seemingly unaware of the connection between money and their ability to express ideas freely in the political arena through the media, largely favor limiting both financial contributions to and expenditures by candidates for national office.

A few months before passage of the Bipartisan Campaign Reform Act (BCRA) legislation in 2002 a Gallup poll asked, "Based on what you have heard or read, do you favor or oppose Congress passing new campaign finance laws?" Seventy-two percent responded that they favored such legislation, up 7 percent from the year before (the rise attributed to the Enron scandal).[1]

Interestingly, this irrational aversion to money in politics cuts across party lines. The poll also found Democrats (77 percent) were only slightly more likely to favor new laws than were Republicans (70 percent) and independents (70 percent). When asked, however, if changing new campaign finance laws could succeed in reducing the power of special interests, 67 percent believed not. A poll from the previous year (2001) showed similar results. In that poll only 22 percent of people believed campaign finance reform legislation would make our democratic form of government work "much better." Thirty-seven percent believed the situation would be "a little better," and 32 percent believed it would remain "about the same."[2] So while a large majority of people said they are in favor of reform, less than a third thought it would really improve our political system. And when asked open-ended questions about what issues facing the country are the most important, people consistently rate campaign finance reform near the bottom.

Historically, when asked explicitly about campaign finance regulation, people have thought that limiting campaign contributions and spending sounded like a good idea. In the 1930s and 1940s, it wasn't just big business contributions people were concerned about. A 1939 poll found that 62 percent of people believed employees of the federal government should be prohibited from contributing money to a political campaign, and 78 percent believed that any person on relief (welfare) should be likewise prohibited. A 1943 poll showed that 65 percent of people believed that labor unions should not be allowed to give money to the campaign funds of political parties, whereas only 59 percent thought the same about business corporations.[3]

By the late 1960s, polls had begun asking people about campaign spending limits. In 1967, 73 percent of people said they would favor a law limiting the total amount of money that could be spent for or by a candidate in a campaign for public office. Sixty-eight percent were in favor of such a law in 1968. The percentage had jumped to 78 percent by 1970.[4]

It is not surprising that people support "reform" when asked about it in general terms but are hazy about what reforms they think are at stake or necessary. We are, as Americans, a reform-minded folk: we like to tinker, to revise, to improve, to progress, to make better. So opposing "reform" is like opposing "freedom" or "liberty" or "Mom and apple pie." It's just not considered decent to be against reform. Yet we often forget, or are not told, that in most cases, reforms are attempts to address problems, real or perceived, that have been created by the passage of previous reforms. Each reform often seems to leave a "loophole" that supposedly requires yet another law.

In the case of campaign finance reform, neither pollsters nor those polled ever make a connection between such laws and any undermining of our basic freedoms. It would be interesting to see a poll asking people whether they would support campaign finance reform even if it meant giving up certain constitutionally guaranteed freedoms. When the question is framed in this fashion, it might not sound like such a good idea. People might begin to realize that these innocent-sounding proposals for "reform" are often direct attacks on the delicate balance of power the Framers wove into the structure of our Constitution and the sacred principle of citizen sovereignty that is at its heart.

None of us can ignore with impunity the unintended consequences of these governmental actions called "reform." In a very real sense, these actions have created a constitutional crisis. The irony is that almost no one, including a majority of the members of the Supreme Court, perceives it as such. It is not anything like the constitutional crises created by the Alien and Sedition Acts of 1798 (discussed in Chapter 9) or by the Civil War. While not as visible or tumultuous as the ones spawned by those events, the current crisis is just as important and just as dangerous.

On the all-important question of sovereignty, the Founders were quite clear: it did not reside with the federal government or the states; it resided with the people. Yet the High Court and Congress have taken it upon themselves in the name of reform to change this fundamental constitutional precept without "the consent of the governed." In essence the Supreme Court said in its landmark *Buckley v. Valeo* and subsequent BCRA decision that protection from the speculative possibility of the corruption of money is more important than the sovereign right of the people to govern themselves.

Who would be sovereign was the core question the Founders had to answer before formulating the structure of our Constitution. Their answer was simple and direct: the people would be sovereign over themselves. Thus to the Founders, the right to vote was sacred, as was the right to communicate with the voters.

In a later chapter, we will see that in its *Buckley v. Valeo* and BCRA decisions, the High Court first strangled and then buried this basic principle and replaced it with the concept that, while the right to vote is fundamental, the right to communicate ideas and opinions is not. This complete destruction of a founding principle of the constitution must be addressed quickly. For if we lose our grip on self-government, how long can we remain free? And once liberty is lost, it is never easily regained.

The relationship of citizen sovereignty to federal elections is a more important subject than it may at first appear. It lies at the very heart of our representative government. Some of the questions this book explores include the following:

- If citizen sovereignty is the foundation of our constitutional government, should it not take a constitutional amendment to change or alter it?

- Has the U.S. Supreme Court, in its *Buckley v. Valeo* and BCRA decisions, transformed America from a free democracy to a "managed" one?

- Why did the Framers of the Constitution define the method for declaring the time, place, and manner of holding federal elections but say nothing about the way in which campaigns were to be financed and conducted?

- What are the practical consequences of government intervention in the way political campaigns are financed?

The Framers understood that the only way self-government could be preserved was through a process of competitive elections where open and unrestricted discourse would help educate the electorate while simultaneously selecting leaders. They realized that truth during the election process could only emerge if all citizens and the press had unrestricted freedom of speech. By including the First Amendment in the Bill of Rights, the Framers hoped to create an impenetrable barrier that protected the press as well as *every* citizen's right to free, unrestrained political speech. Free speech was the armor the Framers created to protect citizen sovereignty.

The Supreme Court's *Buckley v. Valeo* and BCRA decisions destroyed this protective armor by declaring freedom of speech, as envisioned by the Framers and guaranteed by the First Amendment, unconstitutional.

It is my hope that once Americans understand the impact that this dreadful action has had on our basic freedoms and how fair and open elections in this country are threatened, there will be a huge public outcry.

This is not a partisan matter. The issue at hand transcends political affiliation and philosophy. It rests at the very heart of our country's founding democratic principles. The data are very clear. The trend toward an America where only the financial elite can be elected to office is undeniable.

To fully document the significance of the crisis at hand, I have compiled extensive information for all federal House and Senate general election races from the Clerk of House of the U.S. House of Representatives and financial information from the official archives of the Federal Election Commission.

But data without context are meaningless. To completely understand the impact of what is happening today, it is important to review the founding principles that drove the original development of the Constitution. It is also critical to understand how the Founders came upon these principles and why they were so important to them. For the most part, they were learned men. To them the past was not dead—it was alive, especially the history of ancient Rome. To the Founders Rome represented the last good example they had of an attempt at self-government, and the expanded concept of citizen sovereignty as established in the Declaration of Independence, the U.S. Constitution, and the Bill of Rights was based in large part on the Framers' desire to avoid the mistakes of the Roman Republic.

Let us next examine some of the sobering parallels between the origins of the Roman Republic's demise and the decline of citizen sovereignty in the United States today.

3 ROME: A FLAWED MODEL

There never was a democracy yet that did not commit suicide.
    John Adams

The Framers of the U.S. Constitution understood that the initial success of the Roman Republic in creating a formidable military force and culture was responsible for "the grandeur that was Rome." But Rome's eventual internal decay, caused by too restrictive a concept of citizen sovereignty, was something the Framers were intent on avoiding. Thus they adopted a much broader concept of citizen sovereignty as the cornerstone of the new nation. As we have seen, Jefferson framed the principle with a few memorable words in the Declaration of Independence, and the Constitution rests squarely on his immortal words.

Among other things, citizen sovereignty meant that no one, especially by virtue of birth or wealth, would enjoy special privileges under the law, as did Roman patricians and, later, English nobility. It also meant that the people and the government were synonymous: that citizens would be both the ruled and the ruler. This principle seems simple enough. But in reality, citizen sovereignty is an extremely complicated concept. It is an idea contemporary Americans, especially members of the Supreme Court, need to understand better.

Looking back over human history, a strong case can be made that the men who signed the Declaration and devised the Constitution made up the greatest assemblage of political minds in history. George Washington, Thomas Jefferson, John Adams, Alexander Hamilton, James Madison, James Monroe, Benjamin Franklin, and a host of others knew each other, argued with each other, influenced each other, and as a group created the most enduring government the modern world has yet seen. In fact, no nation in existence today has a written constitution that predates the United States Constitution.

The intellectual achievements of these men were grounded in the wisdom of the ancients, a heritage from Greek and Roman writers, philosophers, and statesmen. The Founding Fathers grew up in the neoclassical world of the eighteenth century and learned to read classical literature in the original Greek and Latin.

When the time came to establish their own form of government, they undertook the task with historical precedents in mind. They viewed the ancient Roman Republic as a model, albeit flawed, on which to base their own representative democracy. As Thomas Jefferson put it, "In designing the constitution of these United States of America, we have, at various times, sought precedent in the history of that ancient republic [Rome] and endeavored to draw lessons both from its leading ideas and from the tumult and factions which brought it low."[1]

Like many early Americans, the first Romans were tough, primitive backwoodsmen. And like colonial America, prior to its rise to power and preeminence, Rome was ruled by a foreign power. The man who reshaped Roman society and prepared it for future greatness was Servius Tulius, an Etruscan king.

It was Servius who instituted one of the first censuses in history. That census detailed every Roman's obligation to the city: obey its laws, pay taxes, and do military service. But more importantly, the census gave each level of Roman citizenship certain rights. In proportion to their contribution, Roman citizens were given a say in how the city-state was run. Servius helped create a level of organization unheard of in the ancient world. His reforms sowed the seeds of representational democracy and laid the foundation for the creation of the republic, which only emerged after Servius' assassination.

The Roman Republic was the world's first representative government and was based on the premise that citizens, rather than a king or emperor, would govern. The motto of this new form of government was "Senatus populesque Romanus"–"the Senate and the people of Rome."[2] It was a bold experiment in communal government, with rich and poor both agreeing to share power.

Eventually the stratified structure of Roman citizenship and its restrictive concept of citizen sovereignty created internal strife between wealthy and poor farmers. Membership in the senate was restricted to large landowners (patricians), who were Rome's leaders both politically and militarily. Elections in Rome were rigged in favor of the rich. They ran Rome and its expanding sphere of influence with their own interests in mind. With political power concentrated in too few hands, the patricians were in a position to demand a great deal from the small outland farmers (plebeians), who were excluded from holding positions of power. These demands included the payment of taxes and prolonged service in the military. The strain of these ever-increasing burdens eventually became the focal point of smoldering resentment. (American colonists would later voice much the same kind of objections in condemning George III for "taxation without representation.")

These "lesser" citizens of Rome grew increasingly vocal in their protests as an expanding empire demanded more and more of them. As the empire grew, Rome's citizen army ranged farther and farther away from home. Over time, most Roman soldiers came to view themselves as second-class citizens under the control of a privileged elite—hardly a situation that nurtured loyalty. Virtually powerless, these plebeian soldiers began to resent having to serve a Rome that did not serve them. In addition, the troops were so far removed from their roots that the sights and sounds of Rome, their families, and their small plots of land began to seem more like a dream than a reality to them.

Eventually, the *perceived* need to field armies comprised of full-time soldiers prompted the senate to abandon the concept of a citizen army (a fundamental "first principle of Servius") in favor of a professional military. This was a revolutionary decision. Soon enough, the commanding generals of the army, rather than a fading concept of allegiance to Rome, captured the hearts of the soldiers. What were once the legions of a great city-state, composed of loyal citizens, became the generals' private mercenary armies, powerful enough to challenge the authority of the Roman senate.

One general, Lucius Cornelius Sulla, when ordered by the senate to cede control of his troops, refused, attacked Rome, and allowed his men to sack the city. This act merely emphasized the change that had already taken place: Roman troops, so long denied their full rights as citizens, now regarded Rome as a foreign city—and therefore fair game for plundering. During the melee, Sulla was declared dictator and proceeded to hack away at the powers of the tribunes, the elected representatives of the plebeian class, which seriously undermined Rome's traditional system of checks and balances. Sulla's actions set a fatal precedent, and Rome would never be the same.

Following in Sulla's undemocratic footsteps, Julius Caesar would later cross the Rubicon River and take control of the city. The citizens proclaimed him "dictator for life." Shortly after his triumph, members of the Roman senate attempted to repair the damage by stabbing Caesar to death. However, the civil war and anarchy that followed tore the empire apart. After two decades of constant strife, Caesar's adopted nephew, Augustus, emerged victorious and declared himself emperor. This act proved lethal to Rome's democratic ideals. Its proven system of political checks and balances cracked and give way. From that point on, the Roman Republic was officially dead. Rome had gone full circle from king to republic to emperor.

This ancient history constituted Jefferson's "tumult and factions which brought [the republic] low." In a strong, vibrant representative democracy, citizen sovereignty is not restricted to a privileged few. The rights and responsibilities of citizenship are the same for everyone. Subversions of the "first principles" on which the Roman Republic was founded, such as its failure to extend political power to those who bore the heaviest burdens of citizenship and the abandonment of the idea of a citizen army, eventually upset Rome's time-honored system of governmental checks and balances and ultimately led to the downfall of the republic.

4 CITIZEN SOVEREIGNTY: THE DEAREST THING OF ALL

In free governments, the rulers are the servants and the people their superiors and sovereigns.

Benjamin Franklin

All societies, primitive and advanced, rest on assumptions about the nature of government and the governed. These are sometimes codified in a nation's most revered documents, but sometimes they are no more than truths voiced in songs and stories around a tribal campfire. These "first principles" guide the development of a society and determine its destiny. The great civilizations of antiquity such as Egypt, Greece, and Rome had widespread and deeply held beliefs about human nature and basic political principles. These beliefs provided a solid foundation for giving their world both order and meaning.

When first principles are not rooted in a realistic understanding of human nature, are no longer revered and followed, or fail to meet the test of time, a society tends to fall apart, whether quickly or slowly. The classical world offers numerous examples of such societies, including Greece and both the Roman Republic and the Roman Empire. The modern world provides more recent illustrations of societies that followed destructive "first principles" and suffered the consequences. Communist Russia and Nazi Germany are certainly good examples.

To better understand the crisis of political faith America now faces, it is helpful to examine the most fundamental beliefs that were at the heart of the founding of the United States over two hundred years ago.

The first principles upon which the United States of America is based can be seen in American society prior to the Revolutionary War. Democratic principles that became part of our Constitution had been evolving in colonial America for generations. Local assemblies, majority rule, and citizen selection of public officials were commonplace when the second Continental Congress met in May 1776.

At that time, kings ruled both England and France. A czarina in St. Petersburg was "Mother of all the Russias." A sultan sat in Constantinople. A divinely invested emperor governed in Peking. And a shogun was the unquestioned master of Japan. Except for obscure Swiss cantons (i.e., small communal governments in Switzerland), no democratic republic of any consequence had flourished anywhere on earth for almost two thousand years.

With worldwide totalitarianism as a backdrop, a small group of merchants, planters, and lawyers met in Philadelphia to see if they could pry America loose from the grasp of George III and henceforth govern themselves. On June 7, 1776, Richard Henry Lee of Virginia introduced a resolution in the Continental Congress declaring that the united colonies, thirteen in all, "are and of right ought to be free and independent states." Congress scheduled a vote on Lee's resolution for early July, hoping that its passage would convince France to join the anticipated struggle against its ancient enemy England.

The Continental Congress established a committee to devise a "declaration of independence" that all thirteen colonies could support. Benjamin Franklin was asked to write the first draft but refused, saying he did not write statements subject to editing by others, so Thomas Jefferson and John Adams were assigned the task. Adams in turn suggested that Jefferson draft the document because Adams was not well liked and could not write as well as the Virginian. On July 4, 1776, the second Continental Congress adopted Jefferson's Declaration of Independence, and America's great experiment in self-government began.

Subsequently, on November 15, 1777, the Continental Congress adopted the Articles of Confederation, binding the colonies together in a perpetual union. Article II of this document states: "Each state retains its sovereignty, freedom, and independence, and every power, jurisdiction, and right, which is not by this Confederation expressly delegated to the United States, in Congress assembled." Clearly, this article shows the distrust of a powerful central government that the continental congressmen harbored. The separate states, quite different from one another in a number of significant respects, were alike in jealously guarding their "sovereignty, freedom, and independence." In the midst of divorcing themselves from the British monarchy, they were hardly ready to enter immediately into another liaison that would bind them to a higher authority. Their newly won independence was too precious to surrender, even to each other. However, after operating under the Articles of Confederation for six years, the political leaders of the various states realized the Articles' inadequacy and determined to create a firmer association to prevent a slide into anarchy. By 1787, the states were desperate enough to call for a constitutional convention "to form a more perfect Union."

In formulating a new structure of government, the most fundamental issue the delegates had to address was the great question of sovereignty. The answer would establish the foundation of a new union.

Webster's Third New International Dictionary defines sovereignty as "supreme power esp[ecially] over a body politic."

"Who is sovereign?" is the most fundamental question of government. And the corollary questions are:

1. How are rulers chosen?
2. By whose authority do they rule?
3. How much power are they granted?
4. How long do they hold power?
5. Is there any mechanism for changing rulers?

If you had been French and living during the reign of Louis XIV, you would have answered these questions as follows:

1. The king was born to rule. He is the sovereign.
2. He derives his authority from God.
3. The king's power is absolute. As Louis XIV himself put it, "L'état, c'est moi" (I am the state).
4. Kings ruled as long as they lived. Louis XIV reigned from 1643 to 1715, seventy-two years.
5. There was no legitimate means for a people to change rulers. Death alone could provide relief from an inept or tyrannical monarch.

In England, a similar view of governance had prevailed for hundreds of years. Early in the seventeenth century, King James of England wrote the following:

The state of monarchy is the supremest thing upon earth; for kings are not only God's lieutenants upon earth, and sit upon God's throne, but even by God himself are called gods. . . .

Kings are justly called gods, for that they exercise a manner or resemblance of divine power upon earth: for if you will consider the attributes to God, you shall see how they agree in the person of a king. God hath power to create or destroy[,] make or unmake at his pleasure, to give life or send death, to judge all and to be judged nor accountable to none; to raise low things and to make high things low at his pleasure, and to God are both souls and body due. And like powers have kings: they make and unmake their subjects, they have power of raising and casting down, of life and of death, judges over all their subjects and in all causes and yet accountable to none but God only.[1]

The doctrine of divine right of kings was codified by the French theorist Jacques-Benigne Bossuet (1627–1704), who maintained that because the legitimate monarchs were chosen by God through natural procreation, their subjects had no right to share in governmental decisions or to question a monarch's authority. To challenge the actions of a king or queen amounted to rebellion against God.

Whether or not this doctrine was wholly or partially accepted in England during the reign of George III is open for debate. But the British view of their right of absolute power over the colonies is evident in the passage of the Declaratory Act (1766) that asserted that Parliament had the "full power and authority to make laws and statutes of sufficient force and validity to bind . . . the people of America . . . in all cases whatsoever."

Jefferson and the colonists who signed the Declaration of Independence clearly rejected such parliamentary assertions as well as the idea of the divine right of kings. They chose instead the theory of natural rights as defined by John Locke and others. Locke wrote: "The state of Nature has a law of Nature to govern it, which obliges everyone . . . who will but consult it, that being all equal and independent, no one ought to harm another in his life, health, liberty or possessions. . . . The natural liberty of man is to be free from any superior power on earth, . . . to have only the law of nature for his rule."[2]

Freedom, then, is the natural state of human beings. According to Locke, people formed governments to protect their natural rights and their freedom. The Declaration of Independence specifically affirms this idea: "to secure these rights, governments are instituted among Men." Thus when the people create a government and submit to it, they voluntarily surrender a portion of their freedom in exchange for the protection of their rights against the attack of those who would deprive them of an even greater portion.

Under natural law, governments derive their power from the people themselves, who have the right to reclaim that power if it is used improperly. That is exactly what the Declaration of Independence, with its concise yet eloquent statement of principle and list of transgressions against natural law committed by King George III, demanded.

Written by Jefferson, the Declaration addresses the issue of sovereignty in clear, unequivocal language. For this reason alone, it is among the most important documents Western civilization has ever produced: "We hold these truths to be self-evident, that all men are created equal, that they are endowed by their Creator with certain unalienable Rights, that among these are Life, Liberty and the pursuit of Happiness. That to secure these rights, Governments are instituted among Men, deriving their just powers from the consent of the governed."

The Declaration ends with a catalog of ways in which the king had violated the sovereignty of the people. The first of these (and arguably the most important) are instances in which the king had compromised the effectiveness of the people's representative bodies, and hence their right to govern themselves.

In formulating the Declaration of Independence, the Founding Fathers struck upon the most revolutionary idea of the modern political age: citizen sovereignty. It was this unique concept that led them to create an entirely new form of government, a government that would protect individual liberty and endure, they hoped, for all time. In so doing, they transformed themselves and their fellow countrymen from subjects of a King to sovereign citizens of a new independent nation. They would prove to the world that ordinary people could govern themselves, without monarchs or a ruling class.

In addition, by affirming the sovereignty of the people in the Declaration of Independence, the Founders repudiated a belief in the supremacy of the monarch that had given shape and meaning to society since before the Middle Ages. The direct consequence of this action was of course our war for independence, which, at its core, was really a battle between the king and his subjects over their opposing views of sovereignty.

After securing their freedom, the Framers then crafted a whole new concept of government that insured that henceforth power and control would be from bottom to top. The people themselves would forever be the ultimate controlling power, the sovereigns.

This new structure of power was a radical departure from the Old World's aristocratic tradition. Family, titles, and money were no longer to determine fitness to govern. In America, what mattered most in the new constitutional government would be merit and ability. This fundamental change in the flow of power, combined with a focus on an individual's skill and competency rather than heritage or wealth, established the structure of America's electoral political process for the next two hundred years. As we shall see later, this is what makes the Supreme Court's 1976 *Buckley v. Valeo* decision, declaring limits on political contributions constitutional, so tragic. It has had the practical effect of reestablishing the old aristocratic top-down notion of power in America.

After the ratification of their Constitution, as amended, Americans would have a new and different answer to the five questions posed earlier in this chapter as follows:

1. The people would choose their government officials: at the federal level, a president, vice president, two senators from each state, and congressional representatives based on population.

2. Instead of deriving their power directly from God, those who govern would do so through the delegated authority of the people (the sovereigns) in fair and open elections. (It is important to note what seems to be an exception: Because of a political compromise needed to secure ratification, until the second decade of the twentieth century, U.S. senators could be elected by state legislatures. In 1913, an amendment was ratified that mandated a popular vote for senators in every state. The Seventeenth Amendment further reinforced the idea of the people's sovereignty, this time at the expense of the states. Even after 150 years, the direction of power was still flowing from the people to the government.)

3. Contrary to the powers wielded by kings, the power of those elected to serve in the U.S. government was limited in a number of ways: by the sovereignty of the people, by Constitutional checks and balances that made each branch of the federal government subject to the other two, by the division of powers between the federal and state governments, and by a Bill of Rights designed to protect both the individual and the states against a strong central government.

4. In contrast to monarchs' ruling for life, the only federal officials in
   the U.S. government who would serve for life or until retirement
   would be nonelected judges. The rest must periodically come before the people (the sovereigns) for reelection. The president, vice
   president, senators, and representatives must stand for reelection
   after four, six, and two years respectively. Later, the Twenty-second
   Amendment, ratified in 1951, would restrict the president to two
   elected terms in office.

5. Whereas the monarch held absolute power until death, federal
   judges, the president, and the vice president could be impeached
   and removed from office for high crimes and misdemeanors. The
   Senate and House could vote to expel members, and members of
   both houses would have to stand for reelection. But the Constitution
   gave no one, not even Congress or the Supreme Court, the authority to place limits on the sovereignty of the people, especially with
   regard to the election of federal officials.

French historian Alexis de Tocqueville understood the overriding importance of this change in governmental philosophy when, after visiting
the young nation, he wrote *Democracy in America*. In applauding this country he declared that, while the idea of the sovereignty of the people is
habitually suppressed elsewhere in the world, in America it is openly and
unapologetically proclaimed:

> Whenever the political laws of the United States are to be discussed, it is
> with the doctrine of the sovereignty of the people that we must begin. . . .
> In America, the principle of the sovereignty of the people is not either bar-
> ren or concealed as it is with some other nations; it is recognized by the cus-
> toms and proclaimed by the laws; it spreads freely, and arrives without impedi-
> ment at its most remote consequences. If there be a country in the world where
> the doctrine of the sovereignty of the people can be fairly appreciated, where
> it can be studied in its application to the affairs of society, and where its dan-
> gers and its advantages may be foreseen, that country is assuredly America.[3]

It was the American Revolutionary War, de Tocqueville argues, that
united all the colonists and broke down the economic, social, and intellectual barriers that separated them: "The American Revolution broke
out, and the doctrine of the sovereignty of the people, which had been
nurtured in the townships, took possession of the State; every class was

enlisted in its cause; battles were fought, and victories obtained for it, until it became the law of laws."[4]

This new view of sovereignty was still alive and well in November 1863, when Abraham Lincoln delivered his Gettysburg Address. Note that he begins his speech with a reference to the Declaration of Independence: "Fourscore and seven years ago our fathers brought forth upon this continent a new nation, conceived in liberty and dedicated to the proposition that all men are created equal." Subtract 87 from 1863 and you get 1776. So Lincoln is saying here that the nation was "born" with the Declaration of Independence rather than with the Constitution, and his phrase "all men are created equal" is a repetition of Jefferson's famous words.

Lincoln ends the speech by resolving that "government of the people, by the people, for the people shall not perish from the earth." These words clearly reaffirm the idea that the people are sovereign, that they are the ultimate source of political power. (One eyewitness account of Lincoln's delivery claimed that he emphasized the word "people" rather than the preposition in each of the three parallel phrases.)

Lincoln depicts the Civil War as a struggle to maintain the people's sovereignty. Whether or not one agrees with such an interpretation, it is significant that Lincoln uses that argument to commemorate the sacrifice of the Union dead. It is an argument his audience would have understood and approved. In the mid-nineteenth century, Americans still responded to ritualistic appeals to this basic concept.

In the century that followed, however, Americans seem to have thought less and less about the sovereignty of the people as a fundamental principle of their society. Today they have either forgotten, never knew, or have become complacent about the fact that citizen sovereignty is the foundation upon which the Constitution rests. It implicitly grants the people the solemn right to conduct their own elections in their own way, including the right to contribute whatever funds they wish to whomever they choose.

Citizen sovereignty is not only the most important and most basic principle underpinning the Constitution. It is also something the Framers fully expected both Congress and the courts to protect fervently and effectively. Sadly for us all, as Americans' understanding of their own sovereignty began to fade, this basic principle has not been protected.

5 THE CONSTITUTION AND AMERICA'S FIRST POLITICAL CAMPAIGN

Democracy is two wolves and a lamb voting on what to have for lunch.
Liberty is a well-armed lamb contesting the vote.

    Benjamin Franklin

To better understand what is at stake in the debate over campaign finance, let us look next to the history of elections in this country, beginning with what the Framers of our Constitution had to say on the subject. Article I, Section 4, of the Constitution reads as follows: "The Times, Places and Manner of holding Elections for Senators and Representatives, shall be prescribed in each State by the Legislature thereof, but the Congress may at any time by Law make or alter such Regulations, except as to the Places of chusing Senators." This passage reveals what the delegates in Philadelphia grappled with before agreeing to a constitution: how strong would the "national" or "federal" government become? Could it infringe on states' rights? Could the federal government arbitrarily deprive individuals of basic freedoms, as George III had done? And would the people run the government or would the government run the people?

There were two distinct schools of thought. The Federalists (those who favored a strong central government) believed the government they advocated posed no threat to states' rights or individual freedom. The Anti-Federalists (those opposed to a strong central government) feared otherwise.

Eventually, a spirit of compromise prevailed. The delegates gave the states the right to set the time, place, and manner of holding federal elections, but they reserved to Congress the right to override the decisions of state legislatures in setting the time for elections. However, since senators represented their respective states, state legislatures were allowed the exclusive right to set the *place* for senatorial elections without interference from Congress.

In this small and seemingly irrelevant tightrope walking, we see both the Federalists and Anti-Federalists placated. Setting the time, place, and manner of holding elections (as opposed to conducting elections) is a procedural rather than a substantive question, and therefore of lesser consequence. However, the Anti-Federalists saw a principle at work here and were anxious to preserve it. Thus, the states retained the inviolable right to determine the place of senatorial elections. It was, arguably, a minor victory, but one that, to some degree, reaffirmed the rights of the states.

Given the intensity of this particular skirmish, however, small wonder that the deliberation of the delegates on the Constitution as a whole was so prolonged. It lasted from May 1787 through September of the same year. During this entire time Patrick Henry, as a leader of the Anti-Federalists, railed against the proposed constitution. "The rights of conscience, trial by jury, liberty of the press, all your immunities and franchises, all pretensions to human rights and privileges, are rendered insecure, if not lost, by this change so loudly talked of by some, and inconsiderately by others," he told the delegates. "Is this same relinquishment of rights worthy of freemen?"[1]

As it turned out, by expressing his fears in such specific terms, Henry was laying the foundation for the Bill of Rights. Henry maintained that the people currently possessed these rights under their state governments. To agree to a federal constitution that did not likewise protect these liberties (already guaranteed by the Articles of Confederation) was to risk the loss of freedom itself.

THE BILL OF RIGHTS

It became increasingly apparent to the Federalists that the constitution would not be ratified without some language guaranteeing the rights that Henry believed so endangered. Supporters of the constitution and the central government it would create proposed that, as soon as the constitution was ratified, the delegates would immediately amend it to include a bill of rights.

Sam Adams, John Hancock, and other Anti-Federalists did not trust this promise. What if, after ratification, the Federalists went back on their word and charged out of the hall to celebrate, leaving state and individual rights at the mercy of the new government? Faced with this objection, the Federalists accepted a compromise reached by Adams and Hancock. The ratification process would include a written provision that the constitution would become binding only following the adoption of the bill of rights. If this compromise had failed, it is highly probable, if not a certainty, that the constitution would have never been ratified.

As a consequence, the process of *ratifying* the Constitution was just as important as the process of drafting it, if not more so. Therefore, implicitly if not explicitly, the various elements involved in the process of ratification are as much a part of the Constitution as the wording therein.

The ten amendments, as originally drafted, did not apply to the states— whose power the anti-Federalists did not fear. The delegates intended that the Bill of Rights apply only to the federal government, whose potential power they did fear. Many Federalists thought the amendments unnecessary. Yet time has proven them wrong. In recent decades, most Supreme Court decisions have centered on constitutional amendments rather than on the Constitution itself. Indeed when Americans speak of "constitutional guarantees," they usually mean the Bill of Rights and a few succeeding amendments.

THE FIRST AMENDMENT

As in the case of the Declaration of Independence, what comes first is deemed most important. In the preamble to the Constitution, it is "We the People." In other words, we the sovereigns of the new republic. In the Bill of Rights, it is the First Amendment as ratified. This amendment, upon which so much legislation and judicial opinion depends, is both short and simple: "Congress shall make no law respecting an establishment of religion, or prohibiting the free exercise thereof; or abridging the freedom of speech, or of the press; or the right of the people peaceably to assemble, and to petition the Government for a redress of grievances."

This amendment is primarily concerned with the political rights of the people. The clause concerning "the establishment of religion" was intended to protect individuals from having to support a nationally established church. In protecting the right of free speech, the Framers used the term "abridging" rather than "denying," a careful choice of words. It is possible to allow people to speak out on political issues while restricting or "abridging" their freedom to say everything they have in mind.

The phrase "abridging the freedom" is also important because it implies the preexistence of freedom of speech. You can't abridge something that doesn't already exist. To the Framers, "freedom of speech" first and foremost referred to political speech, the voicing of political opinions, the advocacy of political causes, the support of political candidates, and most of all, the expression of political dissent, which today often takes the form of negative campaign or issue ads. While often disliked and vilified, in a free democracy these expressions of free speech are an unavoidable part of a fair and open election process.

Note that the phrase "or of the press" is simply an addendum to the phrase "freedom of speech" rather than a discrete concept worthy of separate consideration, like "the right of the people peaceably to assemble." Why would freedom of the press be so closely associated with freedom of political speech? King George had never abridged the right of English or colonial newspapers to print columns such as Dear Abby or obituaries or sports results. The activity of the press the Framers wished to protect was the publishing of political commentary or political speech.

The tradition throughout Europe had long been one of repression, often extreme repression, of any opposition to the crown. The Framers wanted to make sure that such repression would never happen in America. The freedom to express opposition to the government is specifically what the phrase "freedom of speech, or of the press" in the First Amendment is primarily designed to protect. Allowing a free people to criticize their government and their elected officials at any time, especially during elections, was an absolute imperative to the Founders.

An election was and still is, after all, something more than voting. It involves the political discourse that precedes the vote, with all its trimmings: speeches, debates, newspaper articles and editorials, handshaking, roadside signs, endorsements, banners, parades, barbecues, and all other means that persuade people to vote for one candidate or another. That is mainly what the First Amendment was protecting when it prohibited the federal government from "abridging" freedom of speech and the press.

AMERICA'S FIRST POLITICAL CAMPAIGN

When did the first political campaign in the United States actually take place? When George Washington ran for president? When the first House and Senate members were chosen?

Actually, it took place in the many months following the Constitutional Convention in Philadelphia. The first political campaign in America was over the ratification of the Constitution. This campaign featured two opposing political philosophies: the Federalist and the Anti-Federalist. It also included "issue ads" in the form of publications like the Federalist Papers and colonial "fat cat" donors like Alexander Hamilton, who freely spent money for the printing of pamphlets, brochures, and newspaper ads that supported their side's point of view.

The initial stage of this campaign was the submission of the proposed constitution to the Congress of the existing Confederation. Here, Federalists argued that the existing alliance was weak and ineffectual. The Anti-Federalists countered that any government more centralized than that permitted by the Articles of Confederation would eventually deprive its citizens of freedoms essential to both self-government and individual happiness. The debate was lengthy and ended in stalemate. Neither side could prevail. Finally, it was agreed to send the constitution to the states without an endorsement or rejection.

Next came the election of delegates in each of the thirteen states to attend a special ratification convention. The Framers could have allowed each state legislature to serve as a ratifying body, but they chose not to. State legislators had been elected for a variety of reasons, none of them because of their opinions regarding the adoption of a new constitution. If delegates were specifically elected to decide that issue, then the resultant body would be more representative of the people (the sovereigns under the new constitution).

Citizens of the individual states had to take this election of delegates seriously. Ratification would mean a new form of government; one that some critics said would be as dictatorial as that of George III. If nine of the thirteen original states ratified the document, then it would go into effect. All thirteen would be bound together as a single nation with a much stronger central government than in the past. So Virginians were as interested in the outcome of constitutional conventions in Massachusetts and New York as they were in that of their own.

In some cases, delegates to the state conventions were elected not because they had voiced an opinion on the issue but because they had gained the confidence of their constituents. Others, however, openly expressed their positions on the subject and were elected or rejected because of these opinions. With the task of electing delegates to the state ratification conventions, the campaign to ratify the constitution was well under way. It was the first of its kind in the history of the world.

It was from New York, a state fiercely divided, that the first significant campaign literature (the equivalent of issue ads today) emerged. Three Federalists—Alexander Hamilton, John Jay, and James Madison—wrote a series of eighty-five essays under the name of "Publius," in homage to the Roman chronicler who codified many of Rome's legal principles. These essays were published in two prominent New York state newspapers, the *New York Packet* and the *Independent Journal,* and reprinted in other newspapers, both in New York and elsewhere. The Federalist Papers, while the best known, were hardly the only extended series of essays published during the ratification process. History records some twenty-four other such series. These "issue ads," designed to promote or defeat ratification, appeared between October 1787, shortly after the Philadelphia convention adjourned, and May 1788. Many received wide acclaim, but the Federalist Papers were so admired that they were eventually published in book form in 1788.

The Federalist Papers exhaustively examined all aspects of the Constitution, including questions pertaining to elections. In one, Federalist 10, Madison even discussed "special interests" and whether or not the political speech of such groups should be restricted.[2] It was undoubtedly the first such discussion of so-called campaign finance reform or, rather, the restriction of campaign contributions and expenditures of certain individuals and groups.

Madison might have been talking about the supporters of the Federal Election Campaign Act of 1974 and the Bipartisan Campaign Reform Act of 2002 and the influence of PACs and corporations when he wrote: "Complaints are every where heard from our most considerate and virtuous citizens, equally the friends of public and private faith, and of public and personal liberty; that our governments are too unstable; that the public good is disregarded in the conflicts of rival parties; and that measures are too often decided, not according to the rules of justice, and the rights of the minor party, but by the superior force of an interested and over-bearing majority."[3]

He could have said "the superior forces of rich and influential lobbyists," since what follows would apply to them as well. Instead of denying that such "deep-pocket" forces exert a strong influence on the workings of government, Madison admits that they do:

However anxiously we may wish that these complaints had no foundation, the evidence of known facts will not permit us to deny that they are in some degree true. It will be found . . . that some of the distresses under which we labor, have been erroneously charged on the operation of our governments; but it will be found, at the same time, that other causes will not alone account for many of our heaviest misfortunes; and, particularly, for that prevailing and increasing distrust of public engagements, and alarm for private rights, which are echoed from one end of the continent to the other. These must be chiefly, if not wholly, the effects of the unsteadiness and injustice with which a factious spirit has tainted our public administrations.[4]

Madison was speaking here for union and a stronger central government. Yet he did not oversimplify the dilemmas that representative democracy faces. Nor did he argue that ratification of the constitution would eliminate these problems. Eighteenth-century American advocates of greater centralized power were not motivated by a belief that government could solve all problems through the evolutionary perfection of human nature.

Madison admitted the fallibility of both government and humanity. After all, the latter created and administered the former. Nevertheless, in Federalist 10 he argued that we must run the risks such a condition entails. Special interests will always exist, he said. Get used to them. Don't try to eliminate their influence at the risk of destroying everyone else's freedom. Political freedom is achievable and desirable. Perfection is impossible.

By a faction, I understand a number of citizens, whether amounting to a majority or minority of the whole, who are united and actuated by some common impulse of passion, or of interest, adverse to the rights of other citizens, or to the permanent aggregate interests of the community.

There are two methods of curing the mischiefs of faction: the one, by removing its causes; the other, by controlling its effects.

There are again two methods of removing the causes of faction: the one, by destroying the liberty which is essential to its existence; the other, by giving to every citizen the same opinions, the same passions, the same interests.

It could never be more truly said than of the first remedy, that it is worse than the disease. Liberty is to faction, what air is to fire, an aliment without which it instantly expires. But it could not be a less folly to abolish liberty, which is essential to political life, because it nourishes faction, than it would be to wish the annihilation of air, which is essential to animal life, because it imparts to fire its destructive agency.[5]

The analogy here is powerful and unambiguous. Human life is sustained by air. So is fire. Fire can be dangerous. However, the elimination of air to eliminate the threat of fire would also mean the end of human life. Likewise, freedom is essential to both special interests (factions) and to vigorous political debate. Withdraw freedom from special interests and you destroy political life itself.

Madison continues, "The second expedient is as impracticable as the first would be unwise. As long as the reason of man continues fallible, and he is at liberty to exercise it, different opinions will be formed. As long as the connection subsists between his reason and his self-love, his opinions and his passions will have a reciprocal influence on each other; and the former will be objects to which the latter will attach themselves."[6] Here Madison reminds his readers of another first principle upon which the Constitution rests: the imperfection of human reason. The balance between central government and state governments, citizen sovereignty, the checks and balances built into the three-fold division of the federal government, and the Bill of Rights—all of these elements of the "more perfect Union" Madison advocated were predicated on the assumption that government itself was subject to selfish manipulation by those elected to make laws and administer them. Everybody needed to be watched by somebody else.

That same imperfection, Madison argued, precluded the possibility that all citizens could desire the same ends and therefore agree on all matters of public policy necessary for the common good. Madison dismissed the possibility of an electoral consensus by people who, through reason, could completely transcend their own self-interests. In doing so, he also dismissed some of the more extravagant claims of the Age of Reason and voiced an argument that would be used in later eras to counter the claims of Marxist utopianism. Reason is by no means infallible. It is always vulnerable to self-interest.

To summarize: democracies must always deal with special interests because human beings are, by nature, egocentric and selfish. Reason becomes either the servant or the conspirator of self-interest. A democratic nation cannot expect unanimity from its citizens. And it is dangerous to deny factions (special interests) full access to the political process, since to do so attacks the primacy of freedom itself. Madison lived in a time when oppressive government was still a living memory to every adult American. The Declaration of Independence clearly resonated in the hearts of the people: "We hold these truths to be self-evident, that all men are created equal. . . . That to secure these rights, Governments are instituted among Men, deriving their just powers from the consent of the governed." Madison and the Federalists believed this statement. So did the Anti-Federalists. Their disagreement lay in whether or not the Constitution and the new government it established would "secure these rights" as the Declaration said it must.

In retrospect, we find in the ratification campaign many of the essential ingredients of a contemporary political contest: two major political factions, opposing economic forces, and a period of campaigning. Literally tens of thousands of people were caught up in the process. It was the most extensive debate on government and political principles ever recorded.

Some fifteen hundred delegates gathered at the various ratification conventions. They examined every section, every phrase, every word of the document they were being asked to approve. And in the end, because they had had a fair chance to compete, the losing side accepted the verdict and joined with the winners in the necessary process of governing. When New Hampshire became the ninth state to approve the document, the Constitution was ratified. The elements of this first political campaign became the model for all federal elections that followed.

As we have already seen, "fat cats" like Hamilton contributed large amounts of cash to support the positions they advocated. Ordinary citizens used their personal resources to voice their pleasure or displeasure with the proposed constitution as well. A political commingling of financial resources by the rich, the not-so-rich, and the poor is exactly what the Founders had in mind. The money spent by these concerned citizens was done in any amount they deemed appropriate and without any restrictions. In fact, had the government attempted to silence them by limiting their contributions or expenditures, they would have revolted. Citizen sovereignty was a very precious privilege shared equally by rich and poor.

Both Federalists and Anti-Federalists would have found it unimaginable that latter-day members of Congress or the Supreme Court would dictate the procedures by which the people elected federal officials to public office. Such restrictions were precisely why the Framers drafted the Bill of Rights. In fact, the Federalist Papers were written to reassure Anti-Federalists that just such things would *not* happen at the hands of a powerful central government.

Sadly for America, subsequent Congresses have legislated the unimaginable, and subsequent Supreme Courts have sanctioned such laws.

6 AMERICAN DEMOCRACY AND POLITICAL PARTIES

In framing a government which is to be administered by men over men, . . . you must first enable the government to control the governed and, . . . next . . . oblige it to control itself.

James Madison

America did not invent the concept of political parties. Crude forms existed even in ancient Greece and Rome. They are the inevitable consequence of various economic and social interests competing in the marketplace of ideas. In a totalitarian regime, parties are superfluous, even subversive. Their very existence suggests that party members share special interests, possibly in opposition to the desire and will of the central authority. Under an absolute monarch or dictator, the existence of such groups often constitutes treason.

A rudimentary form of America's two-party political process predates the Constitution, and in their wisdom, the Framers left the eventual formation of factional political groups and their management to the people. The Framers' failure to establish rules governing the voluntary association by citizens in factions, parties, advocacy coalitions, etc. (or even to mention them in the Constitution) is a clear indication that those who attended the Philadelphia convention did not believe the proposed federal government had the right to interfere in such matters.

This reluctance to control partisan politics did not result from an optimistic view that people were basically good and would do the right thing if given a chance. As a group, the Framers believed in original sin, were distrustful of government, and would have agreed with Lord Acton's observations about the corruptive nature of power ("Power tends to corrupt;

absolute power corrupts absolutely"). In fact, the Constitutional Convention debates in Philadelphia were full of warnings about government and tyranny.

Further, both the Federalists and the Anti-Federalists believed too strongly in the corruptibility of rulers (and in the power of freedom) to give government the power to interfere in the electoral process. If the people were to be sovereign, then any governmental interference in that process would mean that the government, rather than the people, would be the ultimate *authority*. These arguments were never made explicitly at the Constitutional Convention. Why should they be? To the delegates, citizen sovereignty was a natural liberty derived from God. They understood this implicitly and never presumed to do more than prescribe how and by whom the time and place of federal elections would be set.

The authority of the federal government to "control the governed" is in the body of the Constitution. The power that obliged government to "control itself" rested with the sovereignty and judgment of ordinary citizens. These two counterbalancing tenets are the foundation of American democracy. Weaken or destroy either one of these fundamental pillars, and democracy in America is weakened or destroyed.

Factions or "parts" or "parties" are inevitable in a nation where the people are sovereign. Russian Marxists tried to eliminate natural conflicts because they thought one party was sufficient to govern the Soviet Union. After all, in a classless society, people did not compete against each other. Why have opposing parties when the Communists, like the monarchs before them, considered the welfare of all citizens in governmental decisions?

In a democracy, a political party is the vehicle used by ordinary citizens to organize and finance the advocacy for their collective point of view. It is a mechanism for building political consensus. Viewed conceptually, a political party is simply a loosely structured association of people drawn together by a common belief in a given set of guiding principles. These guiding principles concern the nature of government, its proper role in the lives of people, and the institutions that make up society. To gain the support of a majority of voters, these principles must be broad enough to accommodate a number of different points of view and to include a wide range of special interest groups.

Many people think of political parties and special interest groups as one and the same. They are not. In fact, they are quite different. Special interest groups are just that: "special" interest groups. They want what they want, and they are not interested in lawmaking per se. Rather, they are merely interested in legislation that affects something within their own narrow area of concern. These groups promote their specific agenda, whether economic or political or geographic or social. If they can persuade public officials to further that agenda, then their purpose has been achieved. Special interest groups have no desire to govern. Instead, they seek favors and privileges from government without exercising any responsibility for other aspects of society.

At election time there is usually much negative talk about "special interests." The dark secret behind these assaults is that politicians denounce only those special interests that support their opponent. Special interests that support a particular politician or point of view are called friends and supporters. Such are the verbal fireworks from all parts of the political spectrum.

In truth, special interests are "special" not because they are sinister but because they represent various groups of real people, tied together by specific attributes. We are all members, at least philosophically, of one or more such groups. Moreover, since every American is a constituent, each of us can be accused to some degree of feasting at the special interest trough. Remember, the term pork is congressional lingo for any project inserted into the federal budget by a member of Congress—outside the normal authorization process—specifically for his or her constituents.

Political parties are really a coalition or collection of special interests. But there is a difference. The essential purpose of a political party is to seek the broad responsibility to govern so that its vision and principles of government are the ones used in developing public policy and passing laws. In order for a political party to get laws passed that conform to its principles and beliefs, it must control the legislative agenda. Control is the ultimate priority (some say the only priority) of a political party. Thus parties nominate candidates to run in elections and usually provide them with money, workers, and expertise. In return for its support during a national or state election, the party asks only one thing of successful House or Senate candidates: that they vote with the party in selecting the leadership of the legislature. After that initial vote, legislators are theoretically free to act in accordance with their conscience and/or the wishes of their respective constituencies.

Only by electing enough like-minded candidates to gain majority control can a political party enact its vision of government. Parties therefore must attract the support of a wide range of special interests. This process of building coalitions *outside* the formal power structure of government is the single most important function performed by America's two major political parties.

In democracies where no one political party is able to forge a majority coalition outside a legislative body—which often happens in countries where there are numerous political parties—then a majority coalition must be built *within* the legislative body. This type of coalition building involves the forging of alliances with the representatives of various competing political parties elected to the legislative body. More specifically, a deal must be struck between a number of competing political parties within the legislative body such that a working majority can be agreed upon which allows for the organization and operation of the whole. Otherwise, nothing can be accomplished legislatively.

This backroom deal making is where public policy and the general welfare of the state are often both hostage and pawn to the power struggle from which a majority coalition eventually emerges. The end product of this power struggle within a formal governmental structure is what is commonly known as "coalition government." Once formed, such governments are inherently unstable. Because they are nothing more than temporary arrangements, they last only as long as the weakest link feels it is in its own best interest to stay involved. If any faction making up the coalition thinks it can enhance its power by forging a different coalition, they will do so in an instant. As a result, the legislative leadership can be overturned in a single vote. This instability is why coalition government is the curse of all forms of democratic government.

Coalition governments are not based on broad governing principles. Instead, they are based on the irresistible temptation of power. It is not only difficult but often impossible to get any significant legislation passed through a coalition government. This paralysis or inability to act is the mirror image of that opposite evil, the tyranny of the majority that runs roughshod over all dissent.

During the process of forging an alliance to gain a majority within a coalition government, too much power is often given to small, radical minorities. Under such circumstances, to stay in power, weak coalition governments inevitably make concessions that neither please the general population nor serve the greater public good.

Democracies with a healthy and vibrant two-party political process do not have to face the daunting task of continually forging majority coalitions to organize and operate legislative bodies. As a consequence, they have governments that are stronger and more stable.

A strong and well-financed two-party political process is the natural safeguard against the vexing problem of coalition governments, a weakness that plagues many countries around the world. Some examples:

- In Russia today, approximately 150 parties are registered to participate in elections. Of this number, twelve are viable enough to get on the ballot and field candidates for the Duma (Russia's congress).

- In contemporary Italy, there are thirteen political parties, four of which have combined to form a center-right coalition known as the Casa delle Liberta (House of Freedom). Another six parties have created a center-left coalition known as the Ulive (Olive Tree). Three parties remain unaffiliated.

- France is likewise fragmented into multiparty factions—ten political parties and one major coalition, the Union pour la Majorité Presidentielle, which consists of three parties. The remaining seven parties are unaffiliated.

- Within the Israeli Knesset (parliament) there are 120 seats divided among nine political parties, with some of these parties controlling as few as 3 or 4 seats. This means that under certain circumstances, these small fringe parties can control the balance of power in the Knesset.

In nations such as these, where a separate party represents each special interest or shade of political opinion, no one party can win a majority in the legislature. As a consequence, competing parties must forge alliances in order to govern.

To date, America's political process has not been seriously infected with this type of instability. Why? Because both the Democratic and Republican parties have so far been strong enough organizationally and financially to hold their own particular clusters of special interests together to conduct campaigns, win elections, and control legislative bodies.

Jointly, the two major parties in America are the dominant competing political protagonists. Together, they represent the highest court in the land, the court of public opinion. As a consequence, each is more than the sum total of its special interests. This has been the genius of the American system, the most successful of all Western democracies.

One of the reasons "reformers" distrust our two-party system is that they have confused the effect with the cause. It's called a post hoc fallacy in logic. They mistakenly conclude that Democrats or Republicans favor certain public policies because certain special interest groups have contributed money to them. Typically, the reverse is true: special interest groups contribute to political parties because the party already advocates certain public policies.

The best possible checks on campaign improprieties are full disclosure and the two-party system itself. The very presence of well-financed, well-informed, and knowledgeable opposition—forever diligent, forever confrontational—inhibits those politicians (or their handlers) who might be tempted to buy votes or otherwise corrupt the electoral process.

Real political corruption (as opposed to *perceived* political corruption) tends to thrive only where, year after year, one party or elected official dominates with little or no opposition. Not only has the two-party system survived and thrived in America, but it has tended to police the electoral process, punishing those who would subvert our democracy and providing a platform for conflicts in public policy debates to be resolved by the voters.

Rarely has the competitive two-party political process seemed inadequate to the occasion. Infrequently, an issue arises that the two major parties fail to address sufficiently, and third parties will emerge. But after incurring these wounds, the system has always been self-healing, with two dominant political parties eventually reemerging. (Notable examples are the Whigs emerging and eventually replacing the Federalists and Republicans emerging and eventually replacing the Whigs.)

Today it is both ironic and tragic that the United States, having provided the best model for newer Western democracies, would deliberately undermine its own two-party political system. But this is precisely what has been done with the passage of sweeping campaign finance reform legislation. The enactment of Bipartisan Campaign Reform Act in 2002 has transferred an enormous amount of financial muscle away from political parties, seriously weakening them. Yet, warts and all, our two-party system has proven over the years that it beats any alternative.

As Winston Churchill said, "Democracy is the worst form of government except for all the others that have been tried." The same can be said for America's two-party political process.

The weakening of political parties allows members of Congress to operate on a more independent basis. While at first blush this might sound good, over time, members of Congress begin to function as free agents, and it gets harder for them to see the point of rallying as a group. Since campaign finance reform makes incumbent members almost impervious to defeat, they will see less reason to compromise. As the two-party political process grows weaker, consensus becomes increasingly difficult to achieve.

Over time, factions will tend to develop around more polarizing points of view. This in turn will lead to more demagoguery and zealotry both on the left and on the right. Such fanaticism ultimately leads to instability. As people acquire more power, they tend to become less reasonable and less willing to make concessions.

Allowed to stand, campaign finance restrictions are likely to lead America gradually toward coalition government or worse.

7 WHAT IS AN ELECTION, ANYWAY?

> I know of no safe depository of the ultimate powers of the society but the people themselves; and if we think them not enlightened enough to exercise their control with a wholesome discretion, the remedy is not to take it from them, but inform their discretion by education. This is the true corrective of abuses of constitutional power.
>
> Thomas Jefferson

Few Americans can precisely define an election. The most important of all democratic institutions, it is perhaps the least understood. Simply stated, an election is a human creation designed to help a society peacefully select officials who will exercise the power to set the rules for everyone else.

The terms election and campaign are often used as synonyms. They are not. An election has a multitude of components. A political campaign is only one important element; not the entire process. Most people believe an election consists of merely pulling a lever or punching out holes or marking an X on a ballot. Actually, it is much more complex, involving two distinctly different phases.

The first phase of an election involves anything and everything designed to influence the decision of the voters, the purpose being to educate and to persuade them to support or defeat a particular candidate or party or point of view. In a contemporary election, this phase includes elements such as fund-raising, speeches, personal appearances, and radio, TV, newspaper, magazine, and Internet advocacy; endorsements by special interest groups; the activities of political parties and political campaigns (direct-mail appeals, voter canvassing, editorials, bumper stickers, yard signs, buttons, videos, get-out-the-vote phone banks); and a host of other activities too numerous to catalog.

The second half of an election includes all aspects of the voting process itself, including the management of election sites, ballot access, candidate certification, voter registration, voting, tabulation, and other attendant activities. While the first phase is educational and controlled by the people (the sovereigns), the second is essentially procedural and controlled mostly by the government.

Though the U.S. Constitution does not specifically mention very much about either phase of an election, both are addressed by it. The educational aspect of an election is covered by the principle of citizen sovereignty and the Bill of Rights. The procedural parts are addressed by specific reference in Article I, Section 4.

While casting a ballot itself is obviously the essential act, the educational activities of an election are crucial. Informed voting requires information, and information, the lifeblood of democracy, is not free. It costs money to accumulate, formulate, and distribute. Without adequate, diverse, and meaningful information, "We the People" would have no idea for whom we were voting or why.

Where freedom of speech is valued, protected, and allowed free rein, there really is *no limit* to the type and volume of information and input available to voters. The open and unrestricted dissemination of information is one of the fundamental strengths of a healthy democracy.

Thomas Jefferson, in his First Inaugural Address, defined what he believed to be "the essential principles of our government." Prominent among these, he listed "the diffusion of information, and arraignment of all abuses at the bar of the public reason."[1] Indeed, Jefferson regarded a well-informed citizenry as an absolute condition of political freedom: "If a nation expects to be ignorant and free in a state of civilization, it expects what never was and never will be."[2]

Make no mistake. A problem with most of the information distributed to voters concerning candidates and issues is that it is slanted in some way to endorse the point of view of the person, group, or entity doing the distribution. Even when a source is consciously trying to be objective, there is probably an unintentional prejudice in the presentation.

Given this distortion, how can a democracy possibly work to accomplish what is best for the nation or state or community? Madison came up with a good answer. Allow the various special interests in our society to compete in the marketplace of ideas, allow the First Amendment full sway, and allow the people to choose the voice that best represents them, their ideas, and policies they advocate.

As a practical matter, Madison's vision can only be realized when the electorate has unlimited and unrestricted sources of information and input that they can sift through as they deem necessary and appropriate. Anything that interferes with this gathering and sorting process undermines the Framers' concept of democracy.

In many respects, the view of elections that both Madison and Jefferson shared was the political equivalent of the laissez-faire economics of Adam Smith. His *Wealth of Nations,* published the same year as the Declaration of Independence, maintained that large numbers of individuals making independent choices will produce a sounder economy than a centralized government making economic decisions for all. So, too, for Jefferson and Madison. Large numbers of voters making independent choices among candidates for public office will produce better government than a king and his privy council. But Jefferson added that in order to elect wise leaders who will practice good government, the people must be well informed. Wisely, he wrote, "The good sense of the people is the strongest army our government can have. . . . [I]t will not fail them."

Yet there is no question that the information put out by political campaign organizations and candidates is deliberately packaged to favor one particular point of view. The rhetoric is, of course, partisan and therefore a distorted or incomplete picture of the candidates and the issues. And of course the commentary of the press is likewise skewed, though often less overtly so. Indeed, dishonest editors and reporters disguise opinion as fact and advocacy as objectivity; honest editors and reporters sometimes do the same thing, concealing their biases even from themselves. In politics there really is not, nor has there ever been, a totally "unbiased" point of view. This has been true since the founding of our republic and before.

This open, unrestrained, and diverse advocacy of self-interest is exactly the kind of combative competition that the architects of our democracy had in mind when they drafted our Constitution. Candidates, political parties, special interest groups, and even the press (including the electronic media today) were expected to thrash out their differences in the public arena. The voters would weigh the rhetorical conflict, however biased, self-serving, nasty, and conflicting, and make their individual decisions. The sum of those decisions voiced at the ballot box would reveal the will of the people.

The Founders believed strongly in the competition of ideas. That's why they set up a democratic republic. They expressly encouraged competition and lots of it: partisan competition, institutional competition, and candidate competition. In the marketplace of public opinion, ideas would be subjected to rigorous competition, and as a rule only the best ideas and the best candidates would survive.

What free speech literally meant to the Framers, then, is the sovereign right of every citizen and citizen group to disseminate and receive any and all information and input that is not treasonous that they might individually or collectively deem appropriate and necessary regarding any political issue, point of view or candidate, without government interference or restrictions.

History is filled with examples of the difference between "fair" and "open" elections and those that are not. In Communist countries and totalitarian states there are elections, but they are neither fair nor open. In such nations, the government is sovereign and completely controls all phases of the election process, including how much and what kind of information gets disseminated to the people. In such counties there is no such thing as competition between candidates. There is no competition of ideas. As a consequence, the people are not active participants in a dynamic election process. Instead, they simply rubber-stamp a preordained outcome.

A fair and open election is a process that permits every faction to have the same chance to compete for votes among the electorate. The Founders were much more realistic than monarchists or communists about human nature, and therefore they were more realistic about government and elections. They acknowledged the inevitability of diversity and wanted differences settled by competition, not by confrontation.

There is nothing sinister about the presence of partisan rhetoric in an election. To some degree, everyone sees the world through egocentric eyes. During an election, most of us look out for our own selfish interests while trying to convince others and ourselves that we are advocates for the public good.

In fact, determining whose point of view and whose self-interest will prevail is the main reason we hold elections. Put in those terms, election campaigns are struggles for power—the power to impose certain ideas and policies on those who disagree, to favor one special interest over another. So the question that lies at the heart of an election is: "Who gets to be boss?"

At the core of human nature is the deep desire of each person to have things done the way he or she wants them done. To the extent that we can satisfy this innate desire in the real world, we have power. This is what power is and what power struggles are all about. People are said to have power if they have the ability and the authority to control others.

Over the centuries, people have used two powerful human institutions to help them force others to conform to their will. One is the organized violence known as warfare. The other is government. Most civilized people prefer debate to physical force, ballots to bullets. But political debates seldom end with one side convincing the other through friendly persuasion.

When the debate is over, often disagreement has only deepened. In an absolute monarchy or dictatorship, the ruler settles the question arbitrarily by using force against those who object too strongly. In a representative democracy, it is the people—through competitive elections—who decide by majority rule. Because everyone has had a fair chance to compete, the losing side generally accepts the final outcome over time. However, such acceptance only occurs when the losing side has confidence in the political system. This trust usually takes decades to develop. But once established, this trust functions as a bulwark against violence. It is another reason competitive elections are so important in a healthy democracy.

Elections and wars have the same end: the control of one faction or party or nation by another. Given the horror of warfare, most people obviously prefer holding elections. An election, then, is really a substitute for war, an alternative solution. Elections are a series of "battles" in which, hopefully, no one is actually killed but losing candidates and ideas are "killed" politically.

In the final analysis, it is only the continual, aboveboard, and unrestrained exchange of thoughts and ideas between candidates, parties, and factions during the election process that leads to long-term stability and accord within a democracy. That's why open and fair elections are so important and why campaign finance reform is *so wrong:* because it hampers the flow of money, limiting the distribution of information, which restricts the exchange of thoughts and ideas, and as a consequence, undermines the process of holding fair and open elections.

In the next chapter, we'll see how a large chunk of personal wealth injected at just the right moment can decide the outcome of a competitive political contest, which is yet another inequity created by campaign finance reform.

8 POLITICAL CAMPAIGNS AND MONEY

Whoever would overthrow the liberty of a nation must begin by subduing the freeness of speech.

Benjamin Franklin

Political campaigns give life and meaning to elections. Without campaigns, the word "democracy" would be a sorry and meaningless abstraction. The democratic process would be ineffectual, indeed all but impossible.

Campaigns present candidates to the public through speeches, commercials, rallies, and the like. They generate brochures, position papers, pamphlets, and even books. They create ads that define their candidates' points of view and attack the opponents'. And they fund and motivate campaign workers and surrogates who speak on behalf of the candidate, often going door-to-door for one-on-one conversations.

THE KEY TO MILITARY AND POLITICAL CAMPAIGNS

The fact that this process is called a "campaign" says a lot about its essential function. Campaign is a military term used to describe the deployment of troops and arms to conquer an enemy. A successful military campaign often gives the victor the power to govern the vanquished (or prevents the vanquished from governing the victor). A political campaign also decides who will govern.

The power that candidates for office seek is just as real and just as formidable as the power that armies seek on the battlefield. Indeed, in the modern world, the democratic process has to a significant degree replaced warfare as the chief means of transferring power.

However, for democracy to work, opposing forces must have the chance to compete for votes. And in the twenty-first century, that means they must have access to communication outlets and money. If voters don't know who the candidates are or what they believe, then "the people" cannot control their own political destiny.

In what is really a war of words, candidates for office must have the opportunity to carry their message to the electorate. If open debate is forbidden or in some way thwarted, then democracy cannot function. And the alternative to a war of words is a war of arms. The medieval conqueror put the point of his sword on the neck of his fallen enemy and said, "Submit or die." A victorious candidate in America today accepts the concession of his opponent and assumes the office without bloodshed.

Every military campaign and every political campaign is unique. Each has its own peculiar mix of strengths and weaknesses. There are no fool-proof sets of rules that can be followed that will ensure victory either militarily or politically. In addition, all campaigns contain an element of uncontrollable risk. And ultimately, both military campaigns and political campaigns are all-or-nothing propositions. There is no such thing as second place. Whether it is a political campaign that takes a few months or a military campaign that takes years, decades, or longer, you either win or you lose. That's it.

Both military and political leaders ultimately prove themselves in the heat of battle. In these arenas, victory or defeat is heavily dependent on human judgment and available resources being effectively utilized.

Despite there being no fixed rules to ensure success in a military or political campaign, there are well-known principles of strategy that, if intelligently applied, can significantly improve the chance for victory. Some of the principles common to both military and political campaigns are the following:

- *The object is to win.* As General Douglas MacArthur once told Congress, "In war, there is no substitute for victory." The same can be said of a political campaign. Finishing a close second is no consolation, just as it was no consolation to Napoleon that his troops fought well at Waterloo. Even if a candidate loses by just one vote, his or her victorious opponent still assumes all the power that goes with the office. That's why politicians attempt to destroy the reputations of their opponents, just as soldiers attempt to destroy their enemies on the field of battle.

- *Campaigns attack their enemies' weaknesses.* If a challenger is to have any hope of penetrating the invisible protective shield of an incumbent (see Chapter 9) or overcoming the power of incumbency, the challenger must attack the weak spots in the record of the incumbent—hence the necessity for negative ads. To deny a candidate the opportunity to attack his opponent at any stage of a campaign is the equivalent of telling a general he can't attack the enemy at his most vulnerable spot.

- *Campaigns rely on deception.* Military campaigns and political campaigns always try to maintain tight security. That's because both rely on subterfuge and deception. They try to keep vital information from the other side and hide their movements to keep their opponent from knowing where to defend or where to attack. Both sides mask their weaknesses and keep their opponents off balance with surprise attacks and propaganda.

- *Campaigns make alliances.* Both military and political campaigns must make skillful use of allies and prevent their opponents from doing the same. World War I and World War II both illustrate this principle. In the First World War, the Allies joined forces against the Central powers. In the Second World War, the Allies were united against the Axis powers. Without a coalition of nations to oppose him, Hitler might have conquered the West. Likewise in a political campaign, the more allies, coalitions, and supporters you can mobilize, the better your chances of victory.

- *All campaigns are wasteful.* Since neither a military nor a political campaign can know precisely what its opponents will do, both must repeatedly make unanticipated adjustments that consume precious resources. Military campaigns are forever abandoning supplies, machinery, and weaponry along the way either to move against the enemy or to affect a swift and successful retreat. These things occur because war is messy and disorganized. Political campaigns are also wasteful and consume precious resources in order to make unanticipated adjustments to unforeseen calamities or to take advantage of fortuitous opportunities. In a political campaign, you can run out of money quicker than a retreating army can run out of rations or ammunition. And a broke campaign is like a starving army, certain to be cut down and defeated.

- *Campaigns must move quickly and decisively.* Sun Tzu said, "Speed is the essence of war." The same can be said of politics. When your opponent stumbles or reveals an opening, you have to act immediately (sometimes within minutes) to take full advantage of the situation. In politics, that means having enough money on hand to put a radio or TV spot on the air the same evening or to buy a full-page ad in the next morning's newspaper. The goal is to move more quickly than opponents can react, cutting off their options. Often victory or defeat hinges on fast, decisive action, fueled mostly by money.

- *Campaigns must have a plan.* After studying the terrain, going over intelligence reports on the enemy, and assessing the strengths and weaknesses of his own force, a field commander devises a strategy to follow in the campaign that lies ahead. A political campaign manager does the same thing by commissioning polls, consulting with political gurus, hiring media experts, and developing and refining cash-flow schedules. In the course of the actual battle or campaign, the general or campaign manager often deviates from the plan, and deviations usually mean the consumption of more scarce resources. That almost always means more money.

- *Logistical support is critical.* No campaign, military or political, should be launched without abundant resources. On the battlefield, a field commander must have enough troops, weaponry, and supplies where and when needed to engage the enemy. A campaign organization must have campaign workers, media consultants, campaign literature, bumper stickers, yard signs, advertising and, above all, cash in the bank to purchase those resources where and when needed.

An examination of these similarities leads to an inevitable conclusion. Successful military campaigns and political campaigns cannot function without the same basic fuel: money.

The candidate may be attractive and the strategy effective, but without an adequate supply of money a political campaign is almost always doomed to failure. Money translates into political speech. Or more accurately, money grants the power to reach voters with a convincing message. It is difficult to defeat an adversary whose resources are substantially greater than yours. It is almost impossible to defeat an incumbent without at least equal if not superior financial resources.

To be sure, money doesn't guarantee victory. Any number of very wealthy candidates have poured millions of their own dollars into their races and lost. So perhaps the first rule of political campaigns should be this: access to sufficient money doesn't guarantee victory, but the absence of it ensures defeat. The exceptions to this rule are few. While it may seem that money should not be so important in elections, it is. This is the great dilemma of money in politics.

Ideally, Mr. Smith should go to Washington because he's the best man for the job, not because his campaign is the best financed. However, the real world doesn't work that way. No amount of demagoguery, wishful thinking, or denial will change the harsh truth. Wisdom and justice have little to do with the outcome of either a military or political contest. Sometimes those with neither on their side end up winning and thus ruling those who possess both.

History provides examples of well-supplied armies being overtaken by seemingly weaker, inferior, and ill-equipped opponents. The same can also be said for political campaigns. But such instances are the rare exception, not the rule. If studied in detail, extenuating circumstances will usually explain why the seemingly weaker opponent won. Human passion, commitment, dedication, and ingenuity are hard to measure and harder still to quantify. But they do exist and they can influence the final outcome of any contest. In addition, in politics as well as in warfare, you can never rule out stupidity. But none of this changes the fact that money is the key ingredient for success in most political and military struggles.

In a political campaign, money is the all-important resource that makes all other resources possible. Wealthy candidates can spend as much of their own money as they want whenever they feel the need. Nonwealthy candidates cannot. This is the reason an independently wealthy candidate has a significant advantage over one who is not. The arbitrary contribution limits imposed by campaign finance reform have the practical effect of restricting, as well as dictating, how much money a nonwealthy candidate has available and when—no matter what the need. Thus, a wealthy candidate almost always has an advantage.

THE JOHN KERRY CAMPAIGN

In December 2003, during the early stages of 2004 presidential primary campaign, Senator John Kerry was mired in a crowded field with the support of only 9 percent of Democrats nationally. He was running a distant third in Iowa and was over 30 percentage points behind in New Hampshire, his cash reserves were running low, and his campaign was $3.8 million in debt. His fund-raising efforts, like his campaign prospects, were drying up. Early donors may buy the first tank of gas, but they want to see victories before refueling.

Caught in this do-or-die situation, Kerry quietly set up a $6.4 million dollar personal line of credit for his campaign, using his home in Boston as collateral. Immediately thereafter, the campaign borrowed $2.8 million dollars in December 2003 and $3.5 million in January 2004, for a total of $6.3 million just prior to the Iowa caucuses. This quick injection of cash gave Kerry the financial resources he needed to win a come-from-behind victory. His impressive and surprising victory in Iowa set the stage for a first-place finish in New Hampshire, which led to his five-state sweep on February 3 and catapulted him to a commanding 49 percent national standing, which, in less than two months, enabled him to go on to secure the Democratic nomination for president.

While neither Senator Kerry nor his campaign did anything illegal or unethical in setting up a bank loan, this large infusion of cash at just the right moment vividly demonstrates the importance of money in politics, particularly to a campaign that is struggling. (Note: Kerry got all his money back just before accepting the Democrat Party's nomination for president in July 2004.)

And Kerry's loan is hardly unique. Since the Supreme Court's *Buckley v. Valeo* decision in 1976, any number of wealthy GOP, Democratic, and independent candidates have done exactly the same thing. And by so doing, they have put their opponents at a distinct disadvantage.

Table 8.1. Hypothetical fund-raising matrix

Total funds raised	Calls made	Calls answered	Calls completed	$2K donors at 50% donation rate
$2,000	12	4	2	1
$6,300,000	37,800	12,600	6,300	3,150

Table 8.1 shows what it would have taken for one of Kerry's opponents to raise $6.3 million single-handedly by phone, given the $2,000 individual contribution limit mandated by federal election law.

To undertake such a daunting fund-raising task would require the use of "prospecting lists." These are lists of prior donors to other candidates or causes similar to one's own. In prospecting by phone, factors like wrong numbers, answering machines, and busy signals come into play in a significant way. Given these obstacles, it usually takes about three dials on average to generate one answered phone call (i.e., a connected call) and two answered phone calls to make one completed call (i.e., to talk with the person you are trying to reach). Using these numbers as a standard, and assuming a $2,000-donation rate of 50 percent (a very generous estimate), it would have taken one of Kerry's opponents about twelve dials, four phone connects and two completed calls to generate *one* $2,000 contribution commitment.

In other words, for any opponent to match what John Kerry was able to raise with the stroke of a pen, that person working alone would have to average about twenty-four dials, eight connected calls, four completed calls, and two maxed-out ($2,000) contributions every hour, ten hours a day, for more than 158 days. Under the best of circumstances, with everything going right, it would have taken an opponent working full-time including weekends, and doing nothing else, until at least mid-May, to generate on their own a comparable $6.3 million dollars. This, of course, would have been way too late to stop Kerry.

Theoretically, one of Kerry's opponents could have attempted to organize a fund-raising team to help raise the money. But then theoretically Kerry could have done exactly the same thing. But raising $6.3 million prior to the Iowa caucuses, which were less than six weeks away, would have been a herculean accomplishment for any candidate in a hotly contested race given the two-thousand-dollar contribution limit. Kerry's instant loan undoubtedly gave his campaign a huge financial advantage.

Given that Kerry's campaign was out of money and seemed on the verge of collapsing just prior to receiving his personal loan, it is clear that the federally imposed contribution restrictions have dramatically, as well as unfairly, increased the importance of personal wealth in political campaigns.

The exact impact of money in the political process may seem, at times, hard to precisely measure. However, historical facts strongly suggest that at every level of politics, "cash is king." Thus contribution limits imposed by campaign finance reform have unintentionally made access to money one of the most important factors in winning elections. Neither personal wealth nor fund-raising expertise should, in and of themselves, qualify or disqualify a person from running for public office. But the truth is, they do.

The key question is not how much money is collected, but how much is in the bank when needed. The availability of an adequate supply of cash *when* and *where* a need arises is the critical factor that usually determines success. That's why limiting the supply and flow of money into a political campaign, which is what campaign finance reform has done, is like limiting the supply of men and weapons in a military campaign. For financially weaker candidates, contribution limits lessen the possibility of victory. As a consequence, placing arbitrary limits on the availability and flow of money in politics weakens rather than strengthens the democratic electoral process because it limits freedom of speech.

It is important to remember what a political campaign buys with its funds. It doesn't buy votes (at least not in an honest election). Essentially, campaign money buys speech, in all its various forms: media consultants; campaign literature; newspaper, radio, and television ads, etc.

If in politics money buys speech, then a question looms large. How can government, in a free society, abridge its collection and, thereby its disbursement, without, at the same time, destroying the rights of citizens to govern themselves?

9 THE PERCEIVED CORRUPTION OF MONEY VERSUS THE REAL CORRUPTION OF POWER

The truth is that all men having power ought to be mistrusted.

James Madison

The United States Capitol, not the White House, is the single most important government building in America. The Capitol is where the important work of our government is supposed to be done. Congress, the engine of our democracy, is housed within its walls. There, legislation is proposed, debated, and passed or rejected.

Because of the high visibility of modern-day presidents, we tend to forget that much of the real story of our country takes place under the Capitol dome. While a president must sign or veto legislation passed by Congress, the authority to make laws resides solely with Congress. This is just as the Framers of our Constitution intended. Congress is the institution where elected citizens represent their peers. Congress is the cornerstone of our democracy. It was meant to be, and still is, the heart and soul of our government.

The Framers designed the Senate to allow for representation of the often diverse interests of individual states and the House of Representatives to represent and protect the rights of more localized constituencies.

From the beginning, our elections have been carried out implicitly if not explicitly through a competitive two-sided political process. Initially the struggle was more philosophical; that is, no discernable political structures existed. Later it became a more formalized factional or regional partisan competition. But the goal of American democracy has always been to have open and fair elections that offered ordinary citizens a chance to get elected to Congress.

In America, we have always believed that public office is open to the poor as well as the rich. In fact, candidates have often boasted that they came from humble beginnings, knew hunger and deprivation, or were born in a log cabin. For instance, during the 2004 presidential primaries, Senator John Edwards emphasized that he was the son of a mill worker and the first in his family to go to college, Wesley Clark reminded people of his upbringing in a family of modest means, and Dick Gephardt often made reference to his blue-collar heritage. Such statements appeal to our nation's democratic sensibilities and the belief that anyone, regardless of origins, can hold high office.

The Founding Fathers knew that the people elected to office were fallible and, therefore, that any form of government was flawed. Yet, other than establishing who has the authority to set dates and places of elections, they chose to say nothing in the body of the Constitution on the subject of elections. Instead they left that subject to the people. Besides laying out the fundamental structure and specifying duties, they included in the Constitution checks and balances, the Bill of Rights and citizen sovereignty. These constitutional components are really an elaborate set of self-correcting compromises set in place by the Framers as counterweights to keep the whole configuration from getting out of balance, especially the power of the federal government.

SIMILAR THREATS

To better understand the seriousness of the threat now facing our cherished election process and the principle of citizen sovereignty, it may be helpful to remember an earlier threat that occurred shortly after the founding of our republic.

In 1798, when America was facing the *perceived* threat of a hostile invasion from revolutionary France, Congress passed the Alien and Sedition Acts. These laws claimed for government the power to arrest and deport any alien. Further, they also made any American who criticized the government liable to arrest, fine, and imprisonment. These acts will forever be an egregious blot on our history, especially considering that the *perceived* threat they were supposed to address proved to be completely unfounded.

In 2002, when America's political process was facing the *perceived* threat of the corruption of political money, Congress passed the Bipartisan Campaign Reform Act (BCRA), which claimed for government the power to ban political parties' use of "soft money" (i.e., contributions from corporations and unions of any amount or from individual donors above a certain amount). BCRA also made groups of citizens, corporations, labor unions, and individuals who criticized a candidate via electronic media within sixty days of an election liable to arrest, fine, and imprisonment.

At first glance, these two acts of Congress seem worlds apart, but careful scrutiny of their intents and consequences proves otherwise. Each was a direct attack on the idea that "free" people have the right to criticize public officials. And both alter the concept of freedom in America as understood by the Founders. This is why it is worth taking a closer look at both.

Alien and Sedition Acts

True believers in citizen sovereignty responded vigorously to the passage of the Alien and Sedition Acts passed in 1798. Consider the resolution passed by the Virginia General Assembly, which stated the following:

> That the General Assembly doth particularly protest against the palpable and alarming infractions of the Constitution, in the two late cases of the "Alien and Sedition Acts" passed at the last session of Congress; the first of which exercises a power no where delegated to the federal government, and which by uniting legislative and judicial powers to those of executive, subverts the general principles of free government; as well as the particular organization, and positive provisions of the federal constitution; and the other of which . . . exercises . . . a power not delegated by the constitution, but . . . expressly and positively forbidden by one of the amendments thereto; a power, which more than any other, ought to produce universal alarm, because it is levelled against that right of freely examining public characters and measures, and of free communication among the people thereon, which has ever been justly deemed, the only effectual guardian of every other right.[1]

The point of the Virginia Resolution and similar resolutions passed by other state assemblies at the time was to hold Congress accountable for violating its constitutional authority. Specifically, it challenged passage of the Alien and Sedition Acts as a violation of the First and Tenth Amendments. The power to banish aliens and arrest citizens for criticizing the government was *not* delegated to the federal government in the Constitution, and the right to criticize public officials was protected under the First Amendment, which guarantees freedom of speech.

One of the reasons Thomas Jefferson decided to enter the presidential contest of 1800 was his outrage over the passage of the Alien and Sedition Acts. When the votes were counted, after one of the dirtiest political campaigns in American history, no candidate had a majority of the electoral votes. It was left to the House of Representatives to pick the next president. After six days and thirty-six ballots, the House was hopelessly deadlocked. When rumors spread that the Federalists might not accept an Anti-Federalist Jefferson victory, the governors of Pennsylvania and Virginia threatened to send their militias to seize the federal capital. To save the union, it fell to Alexander Hamilton to step forward and urge his fellow Federalists to support Thomas Jefferson.

Immediately upon taking office, President Jefferson pardoned all those who had been convicted under the Alien and Sedition Acts. The federal government then refunded their fines, and the acts were repealed or allowed to expire.

Often referred to as the "Revolution of 1800," this was the first election in the history of modern politics in which there was a *peaceful* transfer of power from one dominant political party to another. This orderly transition of power, at a pivotal moment in our country's formative years, validated the concept of citizen sovereignty. It also legitimized the idea that our two-party political process should operate free from government interference. As Jefferson summarized the conflict: "The order and good sense displayed in this recovery from delusion, and in the momentous crisis which arose, really bespeak a strength of character in our nation which augurs well for the duration of our Republic; and I am much better satisfied now of its stability than I was before it was tried."[2]

Bipartisan Campaign Reform Act

The same charge of unconstitutionality that the Virginia Resolution leveled against the Alien and Sedition Acts can also be made against the BCRA or for that matter the Federal Election Campaign Act passed in 1974. Nowhere does the Constitution specify that the federal government has any jurisdiction or authority to regulate the competitive nature of political parties or federal elections.

France never invaded the United States in 1798, although the threat of invasion did appear imminent at the time. Likewise in 2002, the sponsors of BCRA never uncovered a single example of a candidate or office holder whose vote or actions were altered by a campaign contribution. Incredibly, before passing this legislation, the United States Senate never even bothered to hold a single public hearing to ascertain this information.

The Supreme Court with its bare-majority five-to-four decision upheld all the major provisions of BCRA in December 2003 and wrote 119 pages trying to justify the abolition of basic constitutional rights. In making such an important ruling, one would expect some very strong, compelling evidence proving the corrupting influence of large contributions in politics would be cited in the opinion. There is none. Only a single short paragraph of anything that could remotely be called factual support is to be found in those 119 pages, and that paragraph mentions but three controversial allegations, not proof of corruption.[3] What the High Court relied upon for hard evidence was actually only hearsay. Two accusers gave sworn testimony that the examples they cited represented what they *thought* was corruption.

Certainly, corruption in any form is a grave issue and must be addressed. The word *corruption,* as applied to money and our electoral process, essentially implies that money is subverting the honesty and integrity of our political process. It is also called bribery. This is a very serious charge, which has been discredited by the best studies on the subject. For example, Christopher Magee of the Levy Economics Institute of Bard College found that "contributions . . . have a large effect on the election outcome but do not seem to affect . . . policy stances."[4] After examining the available data, Bradley Smith, a noted authority on campaign finance, the author of *Unfree Speech,* and himself a member of the Federal Election Commission, has concluded: "The idea that serious quid-pro-quo corruption exists is simply not supported by the empirical evidence available."[5] After reviewing some forty studies, three social scientists from the Massachusetts Institute of Technology opined that "the evidence that campaign contributions lead to a substantial influence on [congressional] votes is rather thin." It was their view that members of Congress generally followed their political philosophies and constituents' interests.[6]

Indeed, studies of campaign finance such as those just mentioned affirm what common sense dictates:

(1) that donors tend to contribute to candidates who support their position on key issues;

(2) that donors tend to contribute to incumbents who hold important positions in Congress;

(3) that candidates tend to receive various-sized contributions from friends, relatives, and admirers based on their ability and willingness to give;

(4) that donors tend to support candidates from the same political party;

(5) that political parties tend to spend most of their money helping to elect and reelect their candidates; and

(6) that special interest groups tend to support only incumbents and candidates who support their issue or work to defeat candidates who oppose their issue.

No compelling evidence exists that campaign contributions in any amount constitute "bribes" that influence members of Congress to change their votes on crucial issues or to take positions contrary to their conscience or the interests of their constituents.

From the beginning of our republic, bribery has been against the law. Every citizen knows it, and with few exceptions every member of Congress, regardless of political affiliation, race, religion, sex, or ethnic origin, respects this law and scrupulously abides by it. Yes, members of Congress have gone to jail for accepting bribes. But these bribes were generally not campaign contributions. They were personal "gifts" given and received secretly behind closed doors.

So the High Court didn't stop any *real* bribery by declaring BCRA constitutional. Rather it was passed into law and declared constitutional to end what its supporters both on and off the Court believed was the "appearance of corruption."

The Supreme Court first established this line of reasoning in its controversial *Buckley v. Valeo* decision of 1976, in the aftermath of the Watergate scandal. In *Buckley v. Valeo,* the High Court affirmed that "a major purpose of [the First] Amendment was to protect the free discussion of governmental affairs" but used somewhat hazier language in saying: "The Act's [the Federal Election Campaign Act of 1974's] contribution and expenditure limitations operate in an area of the most fundamental First Amendment activities. Discussion of public issues and debate on the qualifications of candidates are integral to the system of government established by our Constitution. The First Amendment affords the broadest protection of such political expression in order 'to assure [the] unfettered interchange of ideas for the bringing about of political and social changes desired by the people.'"[7]

The Court observed that "every means of communicating ideas in today's mass society requires the expenditure of money," thereby tying the right to exercise free speech with the ability to accumulate and spend funds for that purpose. However, the Court made a distinction between the regulation of contributions and the regulation of expenditures:

> The Act's contribution provisions are constitutional, but the expenditure provisions violate the First Amendment.
>
> (a) The contribution provisions [i.e., limits], along with those covering disclosure, are appropriate legislative weapons against the reality or appearance of improper influence stemming from the dependence of candidates on large campaign contributions, and the ceilings imposed accordingly serve the basic governmental interest in safeguarding the integrity of the electoral process without directly impinging upon the rights of individual citizens and candidates to engage in political debate and discussion.
>
> (b) The First Amendment requires the invalidation of the Act's independent expenditure ceiling, its limitation on a candidate's expenditures from his own personal funds, and its ceilings on overall campaign expenditures, since those provisions place substantial and direct restrictions on the ability of candidates, citizens, and associations to engage in protected political expression, restrictions that the First Amendment cannot tolerate.[8]

In other words, the Court declared in its *Buckley v. Valeo* decision that contribution limits are permissible but that government could *not* put a lid on the amount of money a candidate spends on his own campaign or the "overall campaign expenditures" by the candidate or others. In such cases, the First Amendment could be invoked because those expending the money were themselves engaged in the activities of free expression. This line of reasoning holds that there is no limit on what the rich can spend. In practical terms, however, there is a severe limit on what candidates without wealth can raise and, as a consequence, spend.

Curiously, the High Court ruled that a limitation on contributions "entails only a marginal restriction upon the contributor's ability to engage in free communication." Why? Because "the transformation of contributions into political debate involves speech by someone other than the contributor."[9] In commenting on this distinction, Professor Edward J. Erler of California State University in San Bernardino wrote:

The precise distinction made here by the Court defies reason. Contributions to finance the speech of those with whom one agrees or wishes to promote are no less speech activities than if one uses the money for his own speech. If I gave money to someone—say, a young and relatively unknown successor to Abraham Lincoln—who can articulate my political ideas better than I can, these are no less my political ideas than if I gave voice to them myself. The distinction between spending and contributions is not mandated by any known principle of First Amendment jurisprudence and is alien to the Framers' understanding of both property rights and political liberty.[10]

While ruling that restriction of campaign expenditures violated freedom of speech provisions of the First Amendment, the High Court justified the restriction of campaign contributions as follows: "[T]he primary interest served by the limitations . . . is the prevention of corruption and the appearance of corruption spawned by the real or imagined corrective influence of larger financial contributions on candidates' positions and on their actions if elected to office."[11] Thus the Court justified the federal government's right to impose restrictions on campaign contributions to eliminate even the appearance of corruption. But the Court didn't stop there. It went further and dismissed the idea that these restrictive measures must actually correct an existing problem. Such restrictions are justified even if the problem and the cure are "imagined."

This line of reasoning is not only irrational but frightening. Through research, an idea or perception can usually be proved or disproved. But illusionary threats can be neither quantified nor proven. Foolish fancies should hardly be a standard of measurement. Government and politics exist in a universe of real problems and real solutions. To quote James Madison, "What is government itself but the greatest of all reflections of human nature?"[12] Madison is referring to the everyday reality of human nature, not mystical suppositions.

The fictional demons seen by the Court are visions based on ignorance or superstition. They are illusions, and illusions are hardly what the Founding Fathers used in formulating the Constitution. And illusions should never serve as the basis for altering that Constitution, or as the basis for an act of Congress.

In practical political terms, America would have been better off if the Supreme Court and Congress had simply banned all money from our political process. At least then we would all be disenfranchised equally. No one except the mass media would have unrestricted free political speech. Instead, what *Buckley v. Valeo* did was to create a kind of political monetary caste system. Declaring BCRA constitutional only makes the situation more acute.

Under the Court's mandated financial hierarchy, the wealthy privileged few continue to possess all the unrestricted political speech they care to purchase. Everyone else is severely hindered. While no U.S. citizen of the proper age is prohibited from running for Congress, almost everyone, except the wealthy and incumbents, is stripped of the capability to acquire the resources needed to win election to office.

THE INVISIBLE PROTECTIVE SHIELD
AND THE POWER OF INCUMBENCY

What the Supreme Court failed to consider in its unfortunate *Buckley v. Valeo* and BCRA decisions was the invisible shield that naturally protects all incumbent candidates. This shield is often referred to as the "power of incumbency," but it is not the same thing. A protective shield involves certain innate aspects of human nature, while the power of incumbency pertains to the powers inherent in the office itself.

An incumbent's election shield is real and it is measurable. It is what helps protect every incumbent candidate from defeat. Frankly it is neither intrinsically good nor bad. It is simply a fact of life. It is human nature to judge things largely by accepting other people's point of view. Many of us go with the crowd. This human tendency of "getting along by going along" is the foundation of every incumbent's election protection.

Incumbents have already demonstrated in past elections that they are the popular choice. They won. As a consequence, many people are inclined to vote for the incumbent as a known and accepted quantity. The challenger remains "Brand X." This is generally how most people vote unless they are given a compelling reason to do otherwise. Laundry soap or Congressman: to most people it's all the same.

The power of incumbency is different. It encompasses the privileges, perks, and prerogatives that a person holding office enjoys. By virtue of their office, incumbents are entitled to spend government money to meet with and communicate with constituents and help them solve their governmental problems. In addition, incumbents maintain local offices at government expense and hold press conferences both in Washington, DC, and at home that give them significant media exposure. They are also featured speakers at various types of local events and are generally viewed as celebrities by their constituents. These constituents are also the voters.

To have any chance at all of defeating an incumbent, a challenger must first develop the capability both to penetrate the incumbent's invisible protective shield and to overcome the power of incumbency itself. Without the resources necessary to overcome these obstacles, a challenger candidate never really has a chance. It is like trying to break the sound barrier. You can try all you want in a glider or a balloon, but you will always fail. To break the sound barrier you need a sufficient amount of propulsive force behind your effort. In a political campaign that propulsive force is almost always money.

In the *Buckley v. Valeo* and BCRA decisions the High Court unwittingly strengthened every incumbent candidate's invisible shield. When this fortified barrier is combined with the power of the office itself, most incumbents become impervious to defeat.

Equally frightening is that *Buckley v. Valeo* and BCRA also legitimized Congress's power to unilaterally make it harder for a challenger to defeat an incumbent. The Founding Fathers went to great lengths to carefully balance the three branches of government. Each branch had a level of control over the other yet, at the same time, was uniquely answerable to the people. In this highly refined balance of power, Congress was designated the linchpin because it was supposed to be the most responsive to the desires of the people.

But *Buckley v. Valeo* and the Court's ruling on BCRA have permitted Congress to alter this delicate balance of power by condoning the passage of legislation that favored the rights of government over what the Framers regarded as the God-given rights of the people. To be fair, this was not the expressed intent of either of the High Court's decisions or of Congress's passage of campaign finance reform. However, it is without question a major unintended consequence of both. Now it's time for the American people to seriously examine these consequences.

Prior to the passage of BCRA in 2002, national party committees could offset some of the disadvantage created by the Supreme Court's *Buckley v. Valeo* decision by concentrating their limited financial resources, much of which was "soft money" (see Chapter 12), on certain targeted races. But with BCRA's ban on soft money, this financial equalizer has been drastically reduced, if not totally eliminated.

Having sufficient cash available when needed is sometimes a problem for an incumbent candidate, seldom a problem for a wealthy candidate, and almost always an insurmountable hurdle for a challenger candidate without personal resources. In every campaign there are always infinite ways to spend money, but only a finite amount of dollars available. The High Court's decision has crippled nonwealthy candidates' ability to compete. This is not theoretical speculation. As the data presented in Chapters 12 and 13 demonstrate, it is a verifiable fact.

The financial ceiling created by *Buckley v. Valeo* and BCRA has, for all practical purposes, barred nearly everyone in America from winning election to Congress except incumbents and the wealthy. The average citizen simply cannot accumulate the money required for victory. This is a dangerous precedent with ominous consequences, some of which are already measurably apparent, as we will see in later chapters.

Possible exceptions to this general rule are open seats in gerrymandered congressional districts without an incumbent. Such districts are already so heavily skewed in favor of a single party that victory in the primary is often (though not always) tantamount to election, no matter how much money is spent. But even in this situation, personal wealth and the ability to access a significant war chest quickly are still likely to be the most important factors in determining the primary election's outcome.

Certainly, superior financial resources do not always guarantee victory. There are many examples of both incumbents and wealthy individuals being defeated. Individual election anomalies happen. But these exceptions do not change the fact that both *Buckley v. Valeo* and BCRA are superb insulation for incumbents and wealthy candidates against defeat by ordinary, everyday citizens. In truth many if not most incumbent and wealthy candidates who are beaten actually defeat themselves.

AN IMPERFECT SYSTEM

What the Framers of our Constitution feared most was tyranny resulting from the unbridled abuse of concentrated power. They were determined to develop a structure of government that dissipated power as much as possible without making the central government ineffective or impotent. So in designing the Constitution, they divided the responsibilities of government. When they were finished, while no one was completely happy, most were reasonably satisfied. To quote Benjamin Franklin, "[W]hen you assemble a number of men to have the advantage of their joint wisdom, you inevitably assemble with those men, all their prejudices, their passions, their errors of opinion, their local interests, and their selfish views. . . . Thus I consent . . . to this Constitution because I expect no better, and because I am not sure, that it is not the best."[13]

The Framers aspired to create the best governmental structure possible, free from the most oppressive governmental evil facing mankind, the arbitrary and tyrannical abuse of power. When drafting the Constitution, they envisioned a citizen legislature. Most members would serve for a term or two, then return to private life.

They well understood the innate weaknesses of men. They knew power was addictive. They also knew that for some it was an aphrodisiac. That's why they constructed a system that would play power against power, ambition against ambition, and interest against interest. They were willing, as Madison suggested in Federalist 10, to pit faction against faction rather than to impose restrictions on freedom in the selection of their representatives.

What we see now, some two hundred years later, is an abrogation of trust. Neither the Supreme Court nor the Congress is willing to trust either the system or the people. Instead, they have undermined the delicately balanced structure the Framers put into place as a protection against the corruption arising from the abuse of power.

The Founding Fathers understood that eternal vigilance was only part of the price of freedom. They realized that for their system of government to work over the long run, leaders of every generation would have to demonstrate the intellectual maturity to live with certain imperfections. Too much tinkering with the checks and balances they so carefully crafted might threaten the integrity of the whole structure.

SOURCE OF AUTHORITY

The preamble to the Constitution begins with the words "We the People." It is the people who established and ratified the Constitution, setting up a governmental structure that protected their God-given rights. Underlying this concept is the belief that every human being is important because he or she was created by God and endowed by him at birth with certain unalienable rights that no civil authority may expropriate. That is, the Constitution granted no unalienable rights to the people; the people brought those rights into the union with them. Our ancestors fought the Revolutionary War to secure these rights.

Our Constitution is of necessity a skeletal document. To rely only on its few words and ignore all the complementary documents, materials, and events that led up to and, in fact, paved the way for ratification is to negate the essence of its meaning and intent. The elected officials of the government the Framers created are specifically the servants of the people, and the people maintain their sovereign control through a competitive election process. In America, the people are supreme—not the Congress or the High Court. This is the essence of our constitutional freedom, which was supposed to be timeless.

For the executive, legislative, or judicial branch of government to tamper with this most basic, fundamental fabric of our freedom in an effort to save us from ourselves and the "appearance of corruption" of money is to alter the bedrock of American democracy. This action propels us down a dangerous slippery slope toward a much less competitive election process and worse.

Are the advocates of campaign finance reform and the Court so focused on the fear of the perceived corruption of money that they have become blind to the fear of the real corruption of power? Do they not realize that the potential for real corruption becomes more pronounced when elected officials no longer have to worry about being unseated?

The Supreme Court's 1976 and 2003 decisions, if left unchecked, are nudging us toward the day when we will have to deal with the reality of the corruption of power. Therein lies the terrible catch-22 that *Buckley v. Valeo* and BCRA have created for America.

The American people must soon decide if the words in their Constitution have innate, immortal meaning or if they are all simply obsolete symbols to be manipulated and juggled by the Court.

JUDICIAL RESTRAINT

The great justice John Marshall, the fourth chief justice of the Supreme Court, understood that the Constitution set up a democratic republic and that the American experiment in self-government would necessitate judicial self-restraint in order to be successful. While offering an expansive interpretation in *Gibbons v. Ogden,* a New York case involving licensing acts, Marshall refers to the "sovereignty of Congress" in matters of international and interstate commerce, but he also carefully notes that "the wisdom and the discretion of Congress, their identity with the people, and influence which their constituents possess at elections, are in this, as in many other instances, . . . the sole restraints on which they have relied, to secure them from its abuse."[14]

It is too often forgotten that the delegates at the Constitutional Convention on August 27, 1787, near the end of their deliberations, voted to limit the Supreme Court to the review of matters of a judiciary nature. The court's role was to be a narrow one, befitting the fact that this was to be a system in which the people would govern themselves principally through their elected representatives. Marshall believed that the judiciary must be both independent and respectful of the nature of the constitutional system. As he observed, it is the responsibility of the judiciary "to say what the law is."[15]

Contrast Marshall's view of the judiciary with the view expressed by Charles Evans Hughes. In a speech in 1907, the then governor of New York and later chief justice of the Supreme Court stated, "The Constitution is what the judges say it is."[16] The Framers, of course, would disagree. To them such things as our sovereign rights as American citizens to govern ourselves were grounded in a higher authority than either the Supreme Court or the state.

Formally proclaiming this right is what the Declaration of Independence is fundamentally about. In choosing to fight the Revolutionary War, the Founding Fathers were clearly rejecting the idea that Parliament, the king or any other temporal authority had the power to curb their God-given right to citizen sovereignty.

Whether Hughes still held his misguided view of authority at the time he was appointed to the High Court in 1910 is unknowable. However, his statement does reflect the attitude of certain judges who rebuff the notion that any of the words in the Constitution have intrinsic meaning that defy manipulation by the Court or that the Court must exercise self-restraint because certain principles articulated in the Constitution are derived from a higher authority.

Instead of showing restraint, activist justices tend to view themselves as the highest authority on *every* issue and treat the Constitution mostly as an empty vessel into which any meaning can be poured. They prefer to write opinions based on what they think the Constitution ought to mean, given their vision of how our society ought to function, rather than on what they think the Framers intended when they drafted the Constitution. Activist justices are, in effect, using the right of judicial review (a power not found in the Constitution but asserted by Chief Justice Marshall in *Marbury v. Madison*) as a blank check to subvert the Constitution with their own personal point of view.

Buckley v. Valeo and the court's ruling on BCRA are clear examples. They have split the electorate into unequal parts, with some people having more electoral privileges than others. This kind of unjust limitation of citizen sovereignty is exactly what the Framers were determined to prevent. Now, under the High Court's revisionist view of the Constitution, only incumbents and the wealthy elite have ready access to all the financial resources they need. Everyone else must steer their way through a complex web of restrictions and regulations (Title 11 of the Code of Federal Regulations, *Federal Elections,* is currently over five hundred pages and growing) that make it virtually impossible for them to raise enough money to compete for votes. And if candidates without wealth, or their supporters, accidentally slip up, they can be fined and/or sent to jail.

The Court and Congress have forgotten, or more precisely, have abandoned, the first principles on which the republic was founded. Some of the usurpation of citizen sovereignty by both the Supreme Court and the Congress has occurred gradually, almost imperceptibly. But *Buckley v. Valeo* is unquestionably the single most serious blow, with BCRA coming in a close second.

Ironically, in the name of free speech, the High Court saw fit to use the protection of the First Amendment to essentially place pornography beyond the reach of regulation. Yet it could not find the same protection of free speech in the First Amendment for the most fundamental principle supporting our Constitution. This is not only unbelievable—it's absurd.

Instinctively, many citizens are beginning to sense some kind of loss. According to the Federal Election Commission, citizen participation in the voluntary contribution to presidential campaign funding option on individual tax returns has declined from a high of 28.7 percent in 1980 to just 11 percent in 2000—a precipitous drop. No one has convincingly explained this decline. However, polls suggest that the drop reflects not so much disgust over the perceived corruption of politicians as a belief that the individual citizen no longer matters.[17] Participation in the electoral process is seen as an exercise in futility. People seem to be learning that the limits built into our Constitution are being twisted to justify the accumulation of more power by the federal government. They are also beginning to see that our political process is becoming less competitive.

What we seem to be witnessing is a crisis of spirit in the American people, a gut feeling that something sacred in America is dying, that our fundamental freedoms are being diminished, and that our citizen sovereignty is vanishing. Such a belief may in time turn to a people's rage over their political impotence. (It happened in 1776.) The other alternative is for the people to become passive and less inclined to participate in government, to keep it out of their lives. Either road leads to disaster.

Both of these attitudes are manifestly self-destructive. According to the U.S. Census Bureau, since the adoption in 1971 of the Twenty-sixth Amendment, which reduced the voting age to eighteen, the portion of young people ages eighteen to twenty-four who vote has dropped from almost half to less than a third. According to an article in the *Washington Times* on June 21, 2004, a poll conducted on college campuses by the Leon and Sylvia Panetta Institute for Public Policy found that only 35 percent of students think voting can bring about substantial change. In addition, it was found that only 19 percent of American college students think politics is very relevant to their lives, and fewer than one in ten say they had or would volunteer for a political campaign during the 2004 elections.

A refresher course in the origins of our government and the principles that motivated the architects of our Revolution and our Constitution is in order. Time is running short. As the election process becomes less competitive, power becomes increasingly concentrated in fewer hands. With more people feeling left out of self-government, dissatisfaction within the electorate can only grow. What happens if the day comes when words are no longer able to appease this growing resentment?

The Founders were right about a lot of things, but they were dead wrong in accepting Alexander Hamilton's prediction in Federalist 78 that the judiciary would be the "weakest of the three" branches of government.[18] In both its *Buckley v. Valeo* and BCRA decisions the Supreme Court in effect declared the phrase "Congress shall make no law . . . abridging the freedom of speech" in the First Amendment unconstitutional.

10 WE THE SOVEREIGNS, NOT WE THE SUBJECTS

We the people of the United States, in Order to form a more perfect Union
. . . and secure the Blessings of Liberty to ourselves and our Posterity, do
ordain and establish this Constitution for the United States of America.

> Preamble to the Constitution

The introduction, like a preamble to a law, is the Key of the Constitution.
Whenever federal power is exercised, contrary of the spirit breathed by
this introduction, it will be unconstitutionally exercised, and ought to be
resisted by the people.

> James Monroe

Anyone alive on the day the Constitution was ratified would have understood the meaning and significance of James Monroe's statement. The
"miracle of Philadelphia" was still fresh in memory. The people were jeal-
ous of the rights they brought into the union and were still extremely
wary of government. They certainly would have resisted any attempt to
interfere with their right to conduct their own elections in their own way.

Thus when the Framers of the Constitution came to the question of
federal elections, they did so with obvious timidity. The central government they were crafting was ultimately responsible to the people, who,
being sovereign, would elect their president, vice president, and representatives. As a consequence, the men who gathered in Philadelphia felt
reluctant to be too prescriptive about how elections were to be carried out.
On the other hand, they knew that senators and representatives had to be
elected on a schedule; otherwise their terms in office would begin and end
at varied and arbitrary times. So in Article I, Section 2, of the Constitution

they said this about election to the House: "The House of Representatives shall be composed of Members chosen every second Year by the People of the several states, and the Electors [i.e., voters] in each State shall have the Qualifications requisite for Electors of the most numerous Branch of the State Legislature." This passage raises at least three important points:

1. Members of the House were to be elected by the people, because they represented a relatively small group of them at the local level.

2. Representatives were to be elected every two years because the House, more than the Senate, represented the current opinion of Americans at a grassroots level. If some change in opinion were to occur, it would be reflected first in the various congressional districts. Thus the two-year election cycle gave the people the opportunity to reflect a shift in point of view by electing someone new.

3. By allowing the states to set qualifications for voters, the Framers acknowledged that Congress had limited authority to prescribe how elections for the House were to be carried out. The Founding Fathers apparently intended, as the Tenth Amendment puts it, that all other decisions should be "reserved to the States respectively, or to the people."

Since senators were to represent the interests of the respective states, the Framers prescribed a different manner for their election in Article I, Section 3: "The Senate of the United States shall be composed of two Senators from each State, chosen by the Legislature thereof for six years; and each Senator shall have one Vote."

Their final statement in the Constitution on the election of senators and representatives is in Article I, Section 4: "The Times, Places and Manner of holding Elections for Senators and Representatives, shall be prescribed in each State by the Legislature thereof; but the Congress may at any time by Law make or alter such Regulations, except as to the Places of chusing Senators." Clearly this provision was inserted, in part, to ensure a certain uniformity of term beginnings and endings in both the upper chamber and the lower chamber. Note, however, that the Framers did not initially give Congress the right to alter "the Time, Places and Manner of holding elections." Such a move might have been regarded as presumptuous, or even threatening, by the Anti-Federalists and could have jeopardized the ratification of the Constitution.

Instead, the convention delegates merely provided for the possibility of the federal government taking over these very limited responsibilities. As an illustration of the delegates' reluctance to involve Congress in federal elections, they were not even willing to go so far as to include wording that would allow the federal government primary responsibility for synchronizing elections. This is a very important point because it clearly demonstrates that the delegates had grave concerns about the federal government's involvement in the election process. Beyond the limited federal role of setting "Time, Places and Manner of holding Elections" (which initially existed only in potentia), the conduct of those elections belonged to the states and to the people. And it was the people themselves who formed and operated factional political groups, parties, and coalitions, not the states.

Generations of senators, members of Congress, and constitutional scholars acknowledged that the only way the people's control of the electoral process could be altered was by an amendment to the U.S. Constitution. Subsequent to the Bill of Rights, there have only been seventeen additional amendments to the Constitution, seven (41 percent) of which deal directly with expanding the concept of citizen sovereignty. Note that all seven were designed to correct inequalities in the system, and to extend rather than restrict citizen participation in government.

Had Section 4 of Article I of the Constitution (or any other part for that matter) been interpreted to empower Congress more fully in this area, its members, as well as the nation, could have avoided the complicated and lengthy amendment process. In proposing amendments to remedy these inequities, Congress has time and again acknowledged its lack of authority to do so on its own.

The first of these was the Fourteenth Amendment, which was ratified in 1868. Section 1 reads: "All persons born or naturalized in the United States, and subject to the jurisdiction thereof, are citizens of the United States and of the state wherein they reside. No state shall make or enforce any law which shall abridge the privileges or immunities of citizens of the United States; nor shall any state deprive any person of life, liberty, or property, without due process of law; nor deny to any person within its jurisdiction the equal protection of the laws."

The second was the Fifteenth Amendment, which was ratified in 1870. Section 1 reads: "The right of citizens of the United States to vote shall not be denied or abridged by the United States or by any state on account of race, color, or previous condition of servitude." This amendment guaranteed that African Americans, who had just been granted full freedom and citizenship by the Thirteenth and Fourteenth Amendments, would be allowed to vote. It was an affirmation of a right already implicit in the two previous amendments. Yet Congress clearly believed that this right had to be specified. The manner of determining eligibility to vote had been considered a matter for the states to determine, but since southern whites had a vested interest in disenfranchising recently emancipated blacks, an amendment was clearly necessary.

The Seventeenth Amendment also addressed the conduct of federal elections. Ratified in 1913, it altered the method of choosing U.S. Senators: "The Senate of the United States shall be composed of two senators from each state, *elected by the people thereof,* for six years; and each Senator shall have one vote" (emphasis added). This amendment allowed all qualified citizens, rather than merely a handful of state legislators as the Constitution originally prescribed, to vote for U.S. Senators. In proposing this change, Congress again affirmed the principle of citizen sovereignty. It gave to the many a power that was being exercised by the few, sometimes, it was alleged, behind closed doors and at the expense of the public good.

The Nineteenth Amendment, ratified in 1920, gave women the right to vote: "The right of citizens of the United States to vote shall not be denied or abridged by the United States or by any state on account of sex." This amendment prohibited states from denying women the right to vote. The discriminatory nature of the then current practice was obvious. As late as 1920, women were barred from participating in federal elections. Yet, with such a manifest injustice staring it in the face, Congress still did not claim the authority to abolish the practice with a mere statute.

The Twenty-third Amendment, ratified in 1961, gave the residents of the District of Colombia the right to vote for president and vice president:

> The District constituting the seat of government of the United States shall appoint in such manner as the Congress may direct:
> A number of electors of President and Vice President equal to the whole number of Senators and Representatives in Congress to which the District would be entitled if it were a state, but in no event more than the least populous state; they shall be in addition to those appointed by the states, but they shall be considered, for the purposes of the election of President and Vice President, to be electors appointed by a state; and they shall meet in the District and perform such duties as provided by the twelfth article of amendment.

However, this amendment did not give the residents voting representation in Congress. To this day, that is still an unresolved issue.

The Twenty-fourth Amendment, ratified in 1964, outlawed poll taxes, payment of which was a requirement for voting in five states: "The right of citizens of the United States to vote in any primary or other election for President or Vice President, for electors for President or Vice President, or for Senator or Representative in Congress, shall not be denied or abridged by the United States or any state by reason of failure to pay any poll tax or other tax." This amendment (which covers primaries as well as general elections) abolished the poll tax in those five states, thereby extending suffrage to those who were too poor to pay for the privilege of voting. As late as 1962, Congress still recognized that it had no absolute jurisdiction over the conduct of federal elections. Any change of this nature required an amendment to the U.S. Constitution.

The Twenty-sixth Amendment, ratified in 1971, established a uniform voting age for federal elections. Section 1 reads: "The right of citizens of the United States, who are eighteen years of age or older, to vote, shall not be denied or abridged by the United States or any state on account of age." This amendment was passed during a period when the draft was in force and young people complained that they were old enough to fight but not old enough to vote. The states set the age requirement for voting. Addressing growing unrest over the issue, the amendment lowered the age to eighteen, thereby extending the privileges and duties of citizenship to younger Americans.

These amendments inevitably raise questions concerning the passage of restrictions on campaign financing. First, note that five of the seven amendments (the fifteenth, seventeenth, nineteenth, twenty-fourth, and twenty-sixth) involved limitations on the right of *states* to set electoral rules and procedures. Indeed, three of these (the fifteenth, seventeenth, and twenty-fourth) were directed at the inequitable practices of only a few states. The other two of the seven (nineteenth and twenty-sixth), those extending suffrage to women and eighteen-year-olds, affected all or the great majority of states. In all these cases, the federal government has followed the process prescribed by the Constitution for dealing with states' rights while extending citizen sovereignty to former slaves, residents of the District of Columbia, and others.

However, when it came to dealing with the people's sovereign right to elect their government officials, the process changed. The creation of political parties was not federally ordained any more than it was state or-dained. Though both state and federal governments, over the years, have become involved in the way parties operate, the constitutional justification for such involvement is tenuous, if it exists at all.

The U.S. Constitution doesn't mention political parties. Nor do the state constitutions. So who has jurisdiction over them? The Ninth Amend-ment to the Constitution provides an answer. It reads: "The enumeration in the Constitution, of certain rights, shall not be construed to deny or disparage others retained by the people."

This amendment in particular speaks to the issue of citizen sover-eignty. The fact that the Constitution gives Congress the right to set the time and place of federal elections does not "deny or disparage" the right of the people to form political parties, to nominate candidates, and to support them with financial contributions. So the political parties belong to the people. Or they did. This idea is reinforced by the Tenth Amend-ment, which reads: "The powers not delegated to the United States by the Constitution, nor prohibited to it by the States, are reserved to the States respectively, *or to the people*" (emphasis added).

In which article does the Constitution delegate to members of Con-gress the right to control political parties? The answer is it doesn't. It is the state governments that have this right, if any government entity does. However, it must remembered that the Tenth Amendment is not merely a "states' rights" amendment, but also a "people's rights" amendment. In view of the Ninth and Tenth Amendments, it should be clear that in pass-ing restrictions on campaign contributions and the activities of political parties, the federal government (i.e., Congress, with the approval of the U.S. Supreme Court) has usurped the rights of the people.

Why did Congress find it necessary to amend the Constitution in or-der to ensure that blacks, women, and eighteen-year-olds could vote; that the people could directly elect their senators; and that poll taxes were abol-ished? Because these amendments took powers away from the states, and states collect taxes, elect political leaders, and maintain attorneys general with publicly funded staffs. Like sleeping dogs, states—when aroused—can bite. So Congress acknowledged their sovereignty in such matters as the right to vote and took the circuitous route of amending the Constitution rather than engaging in a fight they might lose.

However, when it came to the financing of campaigns for federal office, Congress was less concerned with the rights of the people, even though these rights (as defined in the First, Ninth, and Tenth Amendments and the preamble) were also well grounded in the Constitution. While "We the People" (meaning "We the Sovereigns," not "We the Subjects") established and ratified the Constitution, no provision was made in the Constitution giving "The People" access to public funds to spend on litigation. Thus "The People" had no public pool of dollars, no tax-supported cadre of lawyers, and no special bureaucracy looking out exclusively for their special constitutional interests in elections.

The only entity the people had to defend their political rights were political party organizations, which are only a loose association of highly interested partisans totally reliant on voluntary contributions. Such an entity is no match for the power of Congress when the Supreme Court chooses to turn its back on a constitutional first principle as important and basic as citizen sovereignty.

Further insight on the Constitution and its relevance to the question of citizen sovereignty and election campaigns may be found by considering the Twenty-seventh Amendment, which places a restriction on the ability of members of Congress to raise their own salaries. It reads: "No law, varying the compensation for the services of the Senators and Representatives, shall take effect, until an election of Representatives shall have intervened." The archaic language of this amendment passed in 1992 seems puzzling. It is worth noting that the Amendment was first proposed on September 25, 1789, as one of the articles to be included in the Bill of Rights. At that time, it was ratified by six states—Maryland, North Carolina, South Carolina, Delaware, Vermont, and Virginia. Because three of the other seven states failed to approve it, it was placed on the shelf. After almost two hundred years, it was revived in 1983. On May 7, 1992, it was declared ratified.

The fact that this amendment was originally intended to be part of the Bill of Rights is highly significant. The Framers of the Constitution were suspicious enough of the Congress to consider a measure that would make it difficult for them to raise their own salaries. In effect, the drafters of this amendment did not want to make members of Congress their own bosses, with the power to enrich themselves—hence this proposed a check on their power.

But look what power Congress has accrued in assuming control over political parties and dictating the rules for their own reelection. The same principle is surely involved. Just as a sitting Congress should be forbidden to raise its own salary, so should any Congress be forbidden from setting up barriers to prevent the election of its opponents. In both cases, Congress would be in a position to pass legislation to the personal benefit of all its members.

The Founding Fathers understood the innate weaknesses of men and, therefore, that any form of government was, by definition, imperfect. Experience had taught them to trust the commonsense judgment of ordinary citizens more than the benevolence of elected officials. This is why they decided to put the ultimate control of their new government in the hands of the people. Unfortunately, by the dawn of the twenty-first century, any widespread understanding of this important fact seems to have receded into the background of our collective memories.

THE BEGINNING OF CAMPAIGN FINANCE REFORM AND THE UNINTENDED CONSEQUENCES OF THE PROGRESSIVE MOVEMENT

The seeds of campaign finance reform can be found in the Progressive movement of the early twentieth century. It was not that progressive visionaries like Theodore Roosevelt, our twenty-sixth president, intended to run roughshod over the concept of citizen sovereignty. To the contrary, they probably thought little about the question. They had an optimistic belief that progressive government would improve people's lives. Leaders of the Progressive movement saw themselves as serving the people rather than usurping their sovereignty.

In the 1904 presidential election, Theodore Roosevelt ran on a platform of "clean government." Known for his high-mindedness, he had built a formidable reputation as a reformer. His opponent, Alton P. Parker, decided in the closing days of the campaign that if he could not win, he could at least speak out against the "menace" of corporate campaign funding. His hope was to cause Roosevelt some embarrassment. For in fact, about 75 percent of Roosevelt's campaign war chest came from big business. Standard Oil (owned by John D. Rockefeller) gave him $100,000 and J. P. Morgan gave him $150,000. Each of these sums would amount to some $2 million or more in today's dollars. Because Roosevelt was so widely admired (he defeated Parker in the Electoral College by a vote of 336 to 140), the scandal Parker tried to stir up did not hurt him.

Theodore Roosevelt was arguably the most popular American president since George Washington. The same landslide that swept Roosevelt back into office also elected a Congress with a big Republican majority supporting him. Whatever reforms he and his fellow Progressives wanted to pass, he had the power within his grasp to enact.

Since his fund-raising practices had been so severely criticized during the campaign, he decided to include the prohibition of corporate contributions as part of his progressive reform package that was targeted at restricting the clout and influence of the "captains of industry" (rechristened "robber barons" by Progressives). To many progressives these titans of industry were evil men who threatened democracy itself.

During the closing days of the presidential campaign, Roosevelt wrote a letter to his campaign treasurer, George Cortelyou, stating, "It is entirely legitimate to accept contributions, no matter how large they are, from individuals and corporations on the terms on which I happen to know that you have accepted them: that is, with the explicit understanding that they were given and received with no thought of any more obligation . . . than is implied by the statement that every man shall receive a square deal, no more and no less, and this I shall guarantee him in any event to the best of my ability."[1]

This statement leaves little doubt that Theodore Roosevelt believed large contributions from individuals, corporations, or labor unions were in and of themselves neither bad nor corrupting. In fact, if he had known his proposed legislation to ban corporate contributions would one day lead to a total prohibition of all contributions above some arbitrary amount, he might have willingly accepted full disclosure as a satisfactory alternative.

Roosevelt's December 5, 1905, message to Congress contained no fewer than seventy-five requests for moderately progressive new laws, and the subheading of the opening section was titled "Control of Corporations." Thus the passage of the Tillman Act in 1907—which prohibited corporations from contributing to federal campaigns—was in reality only one of the minor elements on the progressive laundry list of reforms aimed at curbing the power and abuses of men like Rockefeller, Morgan, Henry C. Frick, and Edward H. Harriman. In other words, it was not campaign finance reform per se.

The Tillman Act was the first piece of legislation affecting contributors. It was in the passage of this law that politicians began to lose sight of the original intent of the Framers in an attempt to fix an election system that was not really broken. The act made it "unlawful for any national bank, or any corporation . . . to make a contribution or expenditure in connection"[2] with a presidential, vice presidential, senatorial, or congressional campaign. Note that, like more recent campaign finance reform legislation, the Tillman Act was proposed in response to *perceived* corruption rather than real corruption. No one seriously argued that Theodore Roosevelt, the titular head of the Progressive movement, was in the hip pocket of Rockefeller, Morgan, or anyone else. Indeed, he was known as an adversary of large corporations, and his reputation for integrity and independence may be unrivaled in the history of the U.S. presidency.

The Tillman Act was arbitrary, a barring of one segment of the population from full political participation because of a popular perception of the moment. A federal district court sustained the constitutionality of its prohibition on corporate contributions and expenditures, but the case was never referred to the Supreme Court for final judgment. This is unfortunate, given that the federal government used the Tillman Act to establish a precedent for controlling the conduct of federal campaigns, and in particular their financing.

At the time, the Tillman Act was hailed as a protection of "the little fellow." Unfortunately, as things turned out it was also the first step toward a time when that same little fellow would no longer have any control over an election process that once substantially belonged to him exclusively.

In 1910, the Tillman Act was superseded by the Federal Corrupt Practices Act, which required candidates to disclose some financial information. It also placed a lid on spending by House and Senate candidates. However, the Supreme Court overturned that provision in 1921. They ruled that limits on candidate spending were unconstitutional, an abridgment of free speech guaranteed by the First Amendment.

In 1934, the right of Congress to regulate campaign financing was challenged in *Burroughs v. U.S.* The High Court decided there was a "clear and compelling reason" to protect the electoral process and thus the right of Congress to legislate in this area. This simple yet vague generalization totally ignores citizen sovereignty. Further, it set the stage for congressional jurisdiction over all aspects of federal elections, including campaign contributions.

It can be easily argued that the federal government has a "clear and compelling reason" to be interested in nearly everything. One reason the Framers structured the Constitution and the Bill of Rights as they did was so that the scope of the federal government's areas of interest would be specifically limited. In terms of politics and elections, it was the people, not the government, to whom the Framers gave primary authority and responsibility.

So how did the U.S. Congress get the right to control the conduct of citizens and their political parties in electing their representatives? With the connivance of the Supreme Court, Congress simply sidestepped the Constitution and usurped it. Indeed, some might say that in a shameful betrayal of our Constitution and the Bill or Rights, they stole it.

11 THE CRUX OF THE PROBLEM

The use of money is all the advantage there is in having money.

Benjamin Franklin

To address any problem there may be with money in politics, one must consider its utilitarian value as well as the fallible nature of humankind. Both of these factors are often used by reformers to support their arguments for prohibiting or restricting the flow of money in politics. Of course these same factors can also be used to sustain arguments against democracy itself.

Assuming a person were willing to contribute 1 percent of his or her liquid net worth to politics, a person with a liquid net worth of $1,000 would give $10, whereas a person with a liquid net worth of $100 million would give $1 million. The only knowable difference between the $10 given by a person in with a liquid net worth of $1,000 and the $1 million given by a person with a liquid net worth of $100 million is that the donors' respective liquid net worth is different. As a percentage of liquid net worth, the financial sacrifice for both is exactly the same. Thus the $10 given by a person with a liquid net worth of $1,000 is no more pure than the $1 million given by a person with a liquid net worth of $100 million is corrupting. It is an identical level of sacrifice. Neither person necessarily has a greater level of commitment or a greater desire for reward.

But the fact remains that the $1 million given by the person with a liquid net worth of $100 million has an infinitely greater utilitarian value to the recipient than does the $10 given by the person with a liquid net worth of $1,000. This is the harsh, undeniable reality of money in politics.

Yet the utility of money and human corruptibility are facts of life. The question is how to deal with these two inescapable truths. The Found-

ing Fathers chose separation of powers, citizen sovereignty, and the Bill
of Rights. Proponents of campaign finance reform choose to view the
solution differently. Their relentless push for campaign financing limits is
essentially based on a utopian dream that some new system can be con-
cocted making money meaningless in politics. That system does not exist
and never will.

In a way, reformers are like curious children who've been given a
powerful microscope. They put all the circumstantial evidence under their
reform microscope and study it intensely. And like children, they become
mesmerized by the disturbing defects and in so doing fail to grasp the
underlying principles.

In his book *Life after Reform,* Michael J. Malbin states that reformers
"recognize the First Amendment implications of regulation but place
greater emphasis on the principle of equality and believe that a central purpose of campaign finance laws is to reduce the influence of large donors
and thereby enhance the equity of the political finance system."[1] While this
theory sounds enticing, it lacks convincing empirical support. The truth
is that the overemphasis on equality often creates unintended inequalities.
As George Orwell memorably wrote in *Animal Farm,* "[S]ome animals are
more equal than others."[2] Likewise, under campaign finance reform some
candidates are more equal than others.

To satirize the unfair political favoritism toward the rich in France
under the Third Republic, Anatole France wrote in *The Red Lily* (1894):
"The law, in its majestic equality, forbids, the rich as well as the poor to
sleep under bridges, to beg in the streets, and to steal bread."[3] This is exactly what the reformers have done in banning large contributions from
politics. Obviously a French law forbidding people from sleeping under
bridges hurt only the poor. In America, campaign finance reform hurts
only nonwealthy candidates, particularly challengers.

Elizabeth Drew, a highly regarded journalist and the author of *The Corruption of American Politics,* raises a grim specter of the corruption of money
within our nation's capital. "The culture of money dominates Washington as never before. . . . It affects the issues raised and their outcome."[4]
In her book Drew does cite examples of elected officials accepting illegal
foreign contributions. But such contributions have been against the law
since money became an important ingredient in politics.

Throughout the balance of her 276-page discourse, Drew fails to cite
a single example of an otherwise legal contribution actually buying a leg-

islative favor. Instead, the evidence presented is mostly a multitude of ways money seems to buy access and influence. In other words, what she shows, or attempts to show, is the appearance of impropriety as opposed to the fact of impropriety.

Drew's book typifies the mind-set of most of the proponents of campaign finance reform. They seem to blindly assume that somehow those with money, access, and power overwhelm what is "right" and arrange sweetheart deals for private gain. Reformers refuse to recognize that many political battles in Washington don't neatly line up as "private" versus "public." The real puzzle is more complex and far less sinister. Yet reformers hold unwaveringly to the view that all money in Washington is corrupting, and anyone touching it is contaminated.

The essential fallacy in this perception is that it is based upon the assumption that everyone in Washington does things for one reason and one reason only: money. It has been my experience that Washington is not that mercenary or corrupt, and neither are its politicians. During my thirty-plus years of dealing with political figures, I have found that ideas, principles, and ideology count for something, and often that "something" is significant. In fact, from what I've been able to observe, constituent jobs and political philosophy trump money and access in determining the votes of members of Congress.

THE PASSION FOR POWER

Reformers like Drew wrongly assume that money is the primary goal of politics. It is not. The primary goal of politics is power. Money in politics is merely a means of acquiring power. Money is not what excites most members of Congress. What members of Congress really want is power.

Most representatives and senators come to Congress with an agenda they want to implement. To accomplish their goals, they need to obtain power. It is important to remember that power and money are not the same thing. Money may or may not help you acquire power, and power may or may not help you get money. There are more than enough examples of one without the other.

In business, most entrepreneurs strive to make money. This is their primary focus. Power may be a welcome addition, but it is not the primary focus. In politics, most politicians are primarily focused on acquiring power. Money to most politicians is only a means to that end. The game in Washington is not to acquire money for its own sake but for the sake of power.

If I were asked to pinpoint the essence of the problem in Washington, I would say it is not a matter of money but of power-obsessed *egos* overriding reason. Power is an intoxicating force that can change the personality of those who possess it. Too many don't just use power—they exalt in it. For years I have watched it happen: some newly elected member of Congress gets the first whiff of power and he or she becomes an addict. Like crack cocaine, political power can transform a person. To some it becomes not merely a weapon to wield but a way of transcending reality, a perpetual haze in which an affected politician lives and moves and has his or her very being. We have all read of people, high on crack, who felt possessed by some superhuman force. Politicians, high on power, have similar delusions. And when politicians perceives that they have become endowed with extraordinary, godlike power, they have lost touch with their souls as well as reality and have set the stage for tyranny because, in this state, they only listen to those who tell them what they want to hear.

A NAIVE DREAM

The common thread in the reform arguments seems to center on the idea that if "corrupting" money were stripped from the process, then our politics would consist only of enlightened interplay of the ideas of reasonable people all striving exclusively for the common good of the country. Somehow all the darker aspects would disappear if only big money would disappear. This is a naive dream that conveniently ignores humanity's corruptible nature.

As Madison said, "If men were angels, no government would be necessary."[5] But men are not angels, so some form of government is always going to be necessary. The question is, what kind of government? And how will it function? The Framers had their vision, which has served us well for over two hundred years.

The Founding Fathers were not concerned about King George's wealth. The fact that he lived in a palatial castle, ate the most delicious foods, and drank the finest wines did not bother them. What disturbed the Founders was the king's arbitrary and dictatorial power. His whim was the rule of law. It was not his money but rather his tyrannical, autocratic system of government that they rebelled against. This is why the Founders decided against setting up their own monarchy, why they were so suspicious of any type of strong central government, and why they made the people sovereign over themselves.

MONEY: A WEIRD AND WONDERFUL SUBSTANCE

Another problem within the debate on campaign finance reform is the misconception on the part of some that money is speech. Money, by itself, is not speech any more than it is food, shelter, or medicine. Yet, the only way anyone can access such things in a free society is via money. So while money itself is not speech, the spending of money is the only way free speech can be effectively exercised.

Money is essentially an abstract idea. The only reason it works is because the people using it have trust and confidence in it. The perception of the corruption of money is an intrinsic part of the nature of money. It is something that is always lurking in the background with the potential to contaminate free speech or anything else it touches. Part of the reason for this lingering cloud of suspicion is that the principles of money defy common sense. In fact, the whole concept of money suggests some sort of trick or con game, no matter how pure the motives.

Imagine a quasi-governmental entity, the Federal Reserve, armed with only a government charter creating a seemingly valuable substance (money) apparently out of thin air. To complicate the process and add further apprehension to the mix, the Federal Reserve also creates a second peculiar substance called government bonds, likewise out of what seems to be thin air. What makes the process seem even more bizarre is the fact that Americans treat both these substances like gold and silver even though they are really only paper or perhaps no more than electronic data. While both are backed by the "full faith and credit" of the United States government, whatever that means, conceptually the whole process still looks suspiciously like a huge, legalized pyramid scheme.

Throughout recorded history, governments have debased money and robbed the people of its full value. Money, greed, speculation, corruption, and the perception of corruption have combined in some fashion to cause *every* financial crisis in America's history. During the early years of our republic, the *perception* of the corruption of money killed both the First and Second Banks of the United States. Reformers in the 1820s and 1830s felt that the only way the people's confidence in money could be maintained was by allowing them to redeem it for gold. But in times of uncertainty, this redemption right caused a run on banks and, in turn, bank closures. Such financial panics only increased people's suspicions about money.

Paradoxically, the well-intentioned bank reforms of the early and mid 1800s actually ushered in the very changes the reformers most abhorred, namely an unstable monetary system, speculative boom-and-bust economics, and corruption. The reformers promised a hard money standard based on the value of gold or silver. Instead of hard money, the country got easy credit in the form of wildcat banking (banks that avoided redeeming paper money for gold). Wildcat bankers ruined the very kind of America the reformers most revered. This same kind of reverse consequence is virtually certain to come about for the advocates of campaign finance reform.

The very nature of money promotes the possibility of deceit, evasion, and uncertainty. The point of money is to spend it. Spending generates commerce, which, in turn, creates prosperity. However, prosperity is not a constant. Recessions and depressions are inevitable.

Money is a legal fiction. Its real value is only that of an implied promise that might be broken. In addition, the value of money increases and decreases based on its scarcity. Such uncertainties are another reason a dark cloud of suspicion permanently hangs over money. Add these suspicions to the facts that human nature is fickle and that human beings can be deceitful as well as easily spooked and it is easy to see why the mind-set that sustains the value of money is tenuous. Is it any wonder, then, that when money is considered in light of the imperfection of human nature there is always the potential for the perception of corruption? How could it be otherwise?

The essential problem with money is that as our trust in it grows, it gains power. This power creates desire, and this desire has both positive and negative consequences. Its positive consequences include the fact that money motivates people to be both creative and productive. Its negative consequences include the fact that money can inextricably lead to deceit and corruption or the perception of deceit and corruption.

Laws that increase openness help to reduce or eliminate actual deceit and corruption because they work to curtail definable and demonstrable real-world problems. But laws passed with the hope of reducing or eliminating the *perception* of deceit or corruption are ineffective. No law or court decision can stop human beings from having suspicions about money, or anything else for that matter. The truth is, there will always be people who perceive evil that is not there.

The bottom line is that people and money are hard to trust, and corruption is easily perceived in both. But it is also true that people and power are hard to trust and that the potential for the perception of corruption is likewise inevitable when it comes to power. This is why the Framers put the fundamental power of government in the hands of the people. They knew no form of government was foolproof. They also understood that an all-powerful Congress could do as much wrong as an all-powerful king. They chose to make ordinary citizens the final arbiters of both money and power in politics, not the central government. This is why they made citizen sovereignty the foundation of the Constitution.

It's also why full, complete, and timely financial disclosure is the constitutionally correct approach for dealing with the vexing problem of the perception of corruption of money in politics. Government-dictated schemes to "manage" American democracy, including the imposition of contribution limits, public campaign financing, term limits, free public broadcasting for certain candidates, and other such devices are all illusory solutions.

A less obvious lesson to be learned from the failure of campaign finance reform is the importance of maintaining the integrity of the political structure first established by the Founding Fathers. As in construction, architecture counts when it comes to government. Without exercising due caution and care, changing the basic design can easily weaken the whole structure, which is exactly what campaign finance reform has done to American democracy.

FULL AND COMPLETE DISCLOSURE

The key to maintaining our fair and open democratic political process is to remove the constraints of campaign finance reform and replace them with a process that fully and completely discloses understandable and relevant information about both donors and recipients. As the amount of money given increases, the amount, type, and specificity of the information disclosed about the donor and the recipient must increase as well. To substantially reduce the perception of the corruption of money, the public needs to know why large amounts are given and, equally if not more important, why they are accepted. Were promises made, and if so, what were they?

There also must be significant penalties for lying in such disclosures. The public needs to know who has given to whom, how much, and why, and they need to have this information in a timely and complete fashion. This enables opponents, the press, and the public to expose or dispel any suspicion of sinister motivations that might be lurking just below the surface.

Full disclosure enables all parties involved in the making and receiving of contributions to disclose the facts from their point of view. Unlike arbitrary contribution limits, full disclosure does not undermine the foundation of participatory democracy. However, even full disclosure is not perfect. In some cases, full disclosure can have a negative effect on an organization or candidate's ability to raise money, particularly those outside the current political mainstream. But such situations can be addressed on a case-by-case basis, which is in fact how this anomaly is currently being handled.

A NEW POLITICAL DARWINISM

The problem with most of the campaign finance laws and court decisions supporting them (besides the fact that they clearly violate both the letter and the intent of the Constitution) is that their effects are exactly opposite from their advocates' intent. By prohibiting large contributions, they make each and every regulated dollar infinitely more valuable. In other words, the High Court and Congress have created a political monetary system that recognizes *only* personal wealth and legally sanctioned nonpersonal wealth in limited amounts as currency.

In essence, they have created a new form of political Darwinism: survival of the richest. Incumbents and those with personal wealth have all the advantages. As we shall see in Chapter 12, the wealthy elite control all the personal wealth, and incumbents soak up the lion's share of the allowable nonpersonal wealth. This monetary system denies most candidates access to adequate funding, which makes elections less competitive and therefore less fair. As a consequence campaign finance reform has unwittingly unbalanced the checks and balances created by the Framers. It has eliminated the flexibility, interaction, and free flow of ideas and information needed to allow our unique form of democracy to function.

It is also ironic that one of the inevitable results of this stranglehold on campaign spending is an increase in negative attack ads. It takes a lot of money to educate the electorate about issues. It has been repeatedly shown that it is much easier and cheaper to turn people off than it is to excite them in a positive way. The more a candidate wants to engage in issues, the more expensive the campaign becomes. It takes lots of resources (air time, advertising, money, etc.) to discuss an issue clearly enough to be argued effectively.

Since running a positive campaign is expensive, logic dictates that if a candidate has limited funds, he or she must engage in negative campaigning. There is no way around it. Thus the increase in campaign tactics that many people view as distasteful is an inevitable, albeit unintended, result of attempting to limit campaign expenditures by setting contribution limits.

And so one must ask: "What have the reformers accomplished?" They have addressed a perceived but unproven evil (i.e., money) and in the process, as we'll see in Chapters 12 and 13, have transformed America from a "free" democracy to a "managed" one; incited the emergence of notorious 527 groups, whose stealth smear tactics can hijack the outcome of campaigns; set the stage for terminating our cherished citizen sovereignty and right to free speech; and created an elite ruling class that, because it cannot be unseated from office, will no doubt inevitably engage in real corruption in accordance with the inclinations of human nature. One day, the reformers will have to answer this: at what point did their flawed handiwork begin leading to tyranny instead of freedom?

A well-informed sovereign electorate with the benefit of full and complete disclosure of campaign finances, not an electorate restrained by the lash and the spur of federal power, should be the strength of our unique form of democracy. It is what the Framers intended.

12 SUPREME COURT MANDATES RUN AMOK

The issue today is the same as it has been throughout all history, whether man shall be allowed to govern himself or be ruled by a small elite.

Thomas Jefferson

The central question this book seeks to address is whether, in passing and constitutionalizing campaign finance reform, Congress and the Supreme Court have substantially undermined what the Framers regarded as the God-given sovereignty of the people.

The tables and charts included or referenced in this chapter and the next provide a great deal of detailed information, perhaps more than the casual reader might find of interest. If the data seem abundant, it is intentional. As stated earlier, I have attempted to write what I know, not just offer opinion. In my view, the best way to demonstrate the unintended destructive consequences of campaign finance reform is to provide a compelling amount of relevant supporting quantitative information and facts.

For most readers, a cursory review of a few charts and graphs should suffice to convey the gist of the points I am making. I urge those who remain skeptical to study the tables and charts I have provided more carefully. The data are neither theoretical nor experimental; they reflect what is actually happening in the real world. Their collective message is both sobering and frightening.

Once Americans were deeply concerned about taxation without representation. That concern led to the American Revolution. Today Americans need to become deeply concerned about *elections* without representation, for the foundation of our freedom as a democratic republic is fair and open elections.

America is not a nation in the traditional sense of the term. Neither race, religion, nor ethnicity binds us together. The adhesive that unites our country is written on three pieces of paper: the Declaration of Independence, the Constitution, and the Bill of Rights. America's foundation is a common belief in the ideals expressed in these documents. These principles and ideas are not written in exotic prose that can only be understood by people with high IQs and law degrees. They are written in fairly plain language. There is even a kind of instruction guide in the form of the Federalist Papers to help clarify their meaning.

For the Supreme Court to repeatedly ignore the clear-cut, unmistakable meaning of the wording in these documents in both their *Buckley v. Valeo* and Bipartisan Campaign Reform Act (BCRA) decisions is tantamount to saying "might makes right." This is a dangerous precedent because our bonding as a nation is rather fragile. In truth, our government is still a novel experiment. If the High Court can simply invent a line of reasoning that enables it to sweep aside fundamental constitutional principles that hold us together as one people, how long will it be before we cease to exist as a nation?

What is needed is a renewed judicial commitment to respect the original meaning of these three sacred documents. The Founding Fathers created these documents and swore allegiance to them because the words used mean something. The most sacred document of all is the Constitution as amended. Saying that our Constitution is a living document is the same thing as saying we don't have a Constitution. For rules to mean anything, they must be fixed. The Constitution as written by the Framers set the rules that bind us together. If change be deemed necessary, then the language contained therein should be amended in accordance with the process prescribed.

The High Court's decisions in *Buckley v. Valeo* and on BCRA are constitutional crimes that invite comparison with *Plessy v. Ferguson* (1896). That onerous decision upheld racial segregation on the grounds that "separate" could be "equal." Like Plessy, these two unfortunate court decisions contradict the express language contained in our Constitution and its amendments. And, like Plessy, they must be reversed.

The Founding Fathers believed that the citizenry was indivisible, that no one by virtue of birth or wealth would enjoy special privileges under the law. As Thomas Jefferson said, "The principle of society with us is the equal rights of all. . . . Nobody shall be above you, nor you above anybody—*pell-mell* is our law."[1] With *Buckley v. Valeo* and its decision on BCRA the Court has subverted this fundamental founding principle and stacked the election process in favor of the wealthy and incumbents.

PATRICIANS AND PLEBEIANS

Instead of Jefferson's vision of citizen sovereignty, the Supreme Court, achieving a new high watermark in legal creativity, has recreated the old Roman concept of patrician and plebeian *political* classes.

At the top of the hierarchy is the financial elite. This is that small, fortunate group of 2.1 million Americans with a liquid net worth (excluding personal homes) of a million dollars or more (Figure 12.1). At the bottom of the Supreme Court's revised definition of sovereignty are the 286.9 million citizens in America with a liquid net worth of less than a million dollars. The Court has created a political monetary caste structure with tiered levels of citizenry based on wealth.

Further, this newly created patrician class can no longer commingle any significant amount of its resources with nonwealthy plebeians. Instead, the financial elite may either support or establish political advocacy entities

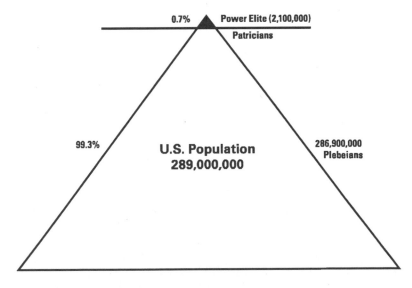

Figure 12.1. America's financial elite and plebeian class
Data from Federal Election Commission (2002) and Merrill Lynch news release (June 17, 2002)

(i.e., 527 groups) outside the conventional competitive two-party system, or they may become candidates themselves and maximize their chance of victory by spending as much of their own money as is needed. In recent elections any number of candidates, particularly Senate challenger candidates, have spent literally tens of millions of dollars of their private funds. In fact, the leadership of one national party committee once stated publicly that it actively seeks candidates who are multimillionaires and can "pay their own way."

According to Anthony Corrado, a campaign finance expert at the Brookings Institution in Washington, of the more than $290 million contributed to 527 groups during the 2004 election cycle, 44 percent of the money came from just twenty-five individuals.[2] These people represent America's newly ordained political elite.

If Congress and the High Court set out to get big money out of politics, they failed miserably. Instead, their actions have made money even more important by devising a system that makes it nearly impossible for citizens without personal wealth to compete successfully. While wealthy candidates can and do accept outside financial help, this does not mean they need it. The only spending constraint on the financial elite is the magnitude of their personal fortune and the amount they choose to commit to politics.

Marx said that when history repeats itself the original tragedy returns as a farce. The Supreme Court's *Buckley v. Valeo* decision and subsequent BCRA decision demonstrate the point. Rather than purge politics of big money, these decisions have gotten democracy out of politics. Success in politics is now virtually the exclusive prerogative of America's new patrician class. Call it a plutocracy, oligarchy, or something else in the making, but a nation that chooses its leaders mostly on the basis of wealth and connections is no longer a democratic republic.

An estimate of the funds controlled by the patrician class in America is roughly $10 trillion, a truly staggering sum of money. To get a sense of the magnitude of this wealth, consider that, as of June 2003, the national debt was $7.4 trillion. The combined wealth of America's patrician class is greater than our country's national debt! It should be emphasized that the $10 trillion figure is only an estimate based on currently available information. But even if this estimate is 50 percent off, the amount of money controlled by the financial elite is still extraordinary. If only a quarter of one percent of this money ($25 billion) were spent on politics during any given election cycle, it would dwarf the sum of all other sources of political funding combined.

The fact that this amount of money is controlled by a small group of people who are forbidden by law to share their wealth has marginalized middle- and lower-income candidates. BCRA has also prevented political parties from making up the difference. The whole electoral process is weakened by the creation of an unpredictable, autonomous financial force outside the established order. This will undoubtedly have a devastating effect on our competitive two-party political process.

Given the prodigious financial muscle of the patrician class, Americans relegated by the High Court to plebeian status might wonder what it takes to become a patrician. The answer to this question is simple and straightforward. All it takes is an accident—an accident of wealth. That accident can occur through birth, marriage, chance, or commerce. Certainly, it is true that chance favors the prepared mind. But even then, chance is still in charge. The exception to this general rule is illegal activity, where malice aforethought is the governing force, and a dangerous force it is. The possibility of someone obtaining significant wealth through white-collar crime, drug trafficking, mob connections, or terrorist activities and then using that wealth to become a powerful political figure in America is surely disturbing. It is also by no means a remote possibility.

Buckley v. Valeo and BCRA put citizen sovereignty on a sliding financial scale. The more personal wealth an individual has, the more sovereignty the Supreme Court allows. The less personal wealth an individual has, the less sovereignty. The Supreme Court has now mandated that the key to political power in America is the accident of wealth. Experience, ability, character, and virtue are no longer the principle qualifications to run for office. Unless you have been struck by the accident of wealth, Congress and the High Court have in effect disqualified you from successfully competing.

Article I, Section 2, Clause 2, of the United States Constitution states: "No person shall be a Representative who shall not have attained to the Age of twenty five Years, and been seven Years a Citizen of the United States, and who shall not, when elected, be an inhabitant of that State in which he shall be chosen." Article I, Section 3, Clause 3, states: "No Person shall be a Senator who shall not have attained to the Age of thirty Years, and been nine Years a Citizen of the United States, and who shall not, when elected, be an Inhabitant of the State for which he shall be chosen."

Neither of these Constitutional Clauses mentions anything about the need for personal wealth as a qualification for election to office. Yet, in *Buckley v. Valeo* and BCRA, the Supreme Court by fiat added personal wealth and/or fund-raising prowess as additional prerequisites for election to office.

CANDIDATE CONTRIBUTIONS

The financial information shown in the tables that follow is compelling evidence that the winning of House and Senate races is substantially (though not exclusively) the prerogative of the financial elite. Yes, on occasion, nonwealthy candidates do win elections. But they are exceptions to the rule. In fact, a careful review of the bottom section of Table 12.1 shows how vulnerable even incumbents without.wealth are when a member of the financial elite decides to challenge them.

These data should be disturbing to those who advocate heightened government control of elections in order to curtail the impact of money. The increase of financial influence coincides with the increase of restrictions. The more Congress and the courts fiddle with the process, the more they empower the very people they say they are trying to bridle. The correlation is uncanny. And the crucial moment in this evolutionary process is *Buckley v. Valeo,* which validated Congress's bold acquisition of additional power over the electoral process.

All the data in Tables 12.1, 12.2, and 12.3 were obtained from either the Clerk of the House or the Federal Election Commission. These tables show the average amount of personal wealth contributed by House and Senate candidates, both winners and losers, for the period 1992–2000, broken down into five categories of competitiveness of races, from "no contest" (races won by 15 percent or more) to extremely competitive (races won by less than 2.5 percent). Money transferred from other campaign committees controlled by a candidate is categorized as part of a candidate's contribution, since the candidate has total control over those funds. Since this source of income is seldom significant, it has not been broken out separately in these tables but can be found at www.money powerandelections.org. As Tables 12.1 through 12.3 indicate, a challenger typically must be not merely a millionaire but a multimillionaire in order to defeat an incumbent.

Table 12.1. Contributions by Senate candidates to their own campaigns, 1992–2000

	MARGIN OF VICTORY					
	≥15%	10%–14.99%	5%–9.99%	2.5%–4.99%	≤2.49%	Total
INCUMBENTS DEFEATING CHALLENGERS						
Winning incumbents						
No. of races	77[a]	9	17	7	4	114
Avg. contributions by candidates	$213,919	$19,500	$208,371	$128,571	$1,578,513	$240,383
Total contributions by candidates	$16,471,760	$175,500	$3,542,314	$900,000	$6,314,053	$27,403,627
Losing challengers						
No. of races	76[a]	9	17	7	4	113
Avg. contributions by candidates	$184,475	$145,751	$1,018,442	$84,829	$7,146,217	$547,115
Total contributions by candidates	$14,020,069	$1,311,763	$17,313,516	$593,800	$28,584,866	$61,824,014
CHALLENGERS DEFEATING INCUMBENTS						
Winning challengers						
No. of races	0	2	3	5	5	15
Avg. contributions by candidates		$3,132,500	$3,928,081	$4,309,403	$2,120,787	$3,346,679
Total contributions by candidates		$6,265,000	$11,784,242	$21,547,016	$10,603,933	$50,200,191
Losing incumbents						
No. of races	0	2	3	5	5	15
Avg. contributions by candidates		$4,662	$0	$471,800	$400	$158,022
Total contributions by candidates		$9,323	$0	$2,359,000	$2,000	$2,370,323

Source: Compiled from data provided by the Federal Election Commission and the Clerk of the House.

Note: To ensure consistency, special elections to fill vacated seats are not included.

[a] John Breaux (D-LA) ran unopposed in 1992.

Table 12.2. Contributions by House candidates to their own campaigns, 1992–2000

	MARGIN OF VICTORY					
	≥15%	10%–14.99%	5%–9.99%	2.5%–4.99%	≤2.49%	Total
	INCUMBENTS DEFEATING CHALLENGERS					
Winning incumbents						
No. of races	1,527[a]	128	95	34	36	1,820
Avg. contributions by candidates	$8,596	$13,116	$24,661	$16,679	$14,627	$10,023
Total contributions by candidates	$13,126,745	$1,678,808	$2,342,763	$567,069	$526,570	$18,241,955
Losing challengers						
No. of races	1,081[a]	128	95	34	36	1,374
Avg. contributions by candidates	$35,213	$98,134	$138,337	$53,915	$117,026	$50,811
Total contributions by candidates	$38,065,066	$12,561,107	$13,141,990	$1,833,119	$4,212,918	$69,814,200
	CHALLENGERS DEFEATING INCUMBENTS					
Winning challengers						
No. of races	5	11	30	20	20	86
Avg. contributions by candidates	$29,378	$58,865	$105,587	$99,040	$160,226	$106,364
Total contributions by candidates	$146,890	$647,512	$3,167,616	$1,980,801	$3,204,512	$9,147,331
Losing incumbents						
No. of races	5	11	30	20	20	86
Avg. contributions by candidates	$24,880	$23,848	$20,180	$34,874	$27,150	$25,960
Total contributions by candidates	$124,400	$262,331	$605,401	$697,476	$542,992	$2,232,600

Source: Compiled from data provided by the Federal Election Commission and the Clerk of the House.

[a]There were 446 races in which the incumbent had no financial opposition. In 68 elections, the incumbent was the only name on the ballot; there were 102 challenger candidates who did not file campaign financial disclosure reports with the Federal Election Commission (FEC), and another 276 filed with the FEC but reported total receipts of $0.

Table 12.3. Contributions by Senate and House candidates to their own campaigns for open seats, 1992–2000

	MARGIN OF VICTORY					
	≥15%	10%–14.99%	5%–9.99%	2.5%–4.99%	≤2.49%	Total
SENATE RACES						
Winning candidates						
No. of races	11	10	7	6	4	38
Avg. contributions by candidates	$292,447	$1,298,818	$12,001	$10,225,690	$84,380	$2,052,125
Total contributions by candidates	$3,216,919	$12,988,181	$84,010	$61,354,139	$337,518	$77,980,767
Losing candidates						
No. of races	11	10	7	6	4	38
Avg. contributions by candidates	$185,692	$79,276	$372,027	$395,097	$1,810,707	$396,130
Total contributions by candidates	$2,042,608	$792,755	$2,604,188	$2,370,581	$7,242,826	$15,052,958
HOUSE RACES						
Winning candidates						
No. of races	128[a]	36	48	33	19	264
Avg. contributions by candidates	$123,018	$63,666	$164,775	$70,846	$123,374	$116,021
Total contributions by candidates	$15,746,295	$2,291,960	$7,909,210	$2,337,927	$2,344,106	$30,629,498
Losing candidates						
No. of races	118[a]	36	48	33	19	254
Avg. contributions by candidates	$63,376	$165,171	$167,154	$252,303	$109,582	$125,417
Total contributions by candidates	$7,478,346	$5,946,166	$8,023,373	$8,325,995	$2,082,066	$31,855,946

Source: Compiled from data provided by the Federal Election Commission and the Clerk of the House.

[a]Ten open-seat winners had no financial opposition. In one of those races the winner was the only name on the ballot; in two other elections the losing candidate did not file with the Federal Election Commission (FEC), and in another seven the losing candidates filed with the FEC but reported total receipts of $0.

SENATE AND HOUSE SUMMARY TABLES

Senate

Between 1992 and 2000, only fifteen incumbent senators were defeated in reelection bids. Challengers spent an average of $3 million of their own money to defeat them. In elections for the thirty-eight open Senate seats during the same time period, the winning candidate spent an average of more than $2 million of their own money. These data make it clear that running for and winning a seat in the United States Senate is very much, although not exclusively, a function of personal wealth.

House

Because of the well-known and time-tested practice of "gerrymandering" congressional districts, determining the precise influence of personal wealth in House races is more difficult than for Senate races. Gerrymandering is the dividing of election districts during the redistricting process in such a way that one political party is given a distinct advantage.

In his book *Monopoly Politics,* James C. Miller asserts that 332 of the 435 seats in the House are secure for one party or the other. This estimate is reinforced by the fact that during the period 1992–2000, 95 percent of House incumbents were reelected, and 84 percent won in a landside victory of 15 percent or more.

So the potent combination of a House incumbent's invisible protective shield and the power of incumbency (chapter 9), head-of-the-line access to regulated "hard" money, and the advantage of a gerrymandered safe district would seem to make most members of the House of Representatives immune to defeat.

Yet the data in Table 12.4 strongly suggest that during the same period, lack of money by challengers, not gerrymandering, was the single biggest reason that the vast majority of House incumbents faced little or no real competition when running for reelection. When challengers raised less than $400,000, as they did in 83 percent of all House campaigns against incumbents, the incumbent won an unbelievable 99 percent of the races. When challengers raised between $400,000 and $1 million, the incumbent won 81 percent of the races, and when challengers raised more than $1 million, incumbents won only 71 percent of the time. As challenger receipts increase, the number of incumbents winning and their margin of

Table 12.4. Challengers' net campaign receipts and margin of victory in House elections, 1992–2000

	CHALLENGERS' NET CAMPAIGN RECEIPTS			
Margin of victory	≤$400,000 (no. [%])	$400,001–$1,000,000 (no. [%])	≥$1,000,000 (no. [%])	Totals (no. [%])
INCUMBENT WINNERS				
≤4.99%	27 [1.7%]	34 [13.5%]	9 [11.4%]	70 [3.7%]
5%–9.99%	42 [2.7%]	36 [14.3%]	17 [21.5%]	95 [5.0%]
≥10%	1,491 [94.7%]	134 [53.2%]	30 [38.0%]	1,655 [86.8%]
Subtotal	1,560 [99.1%]	204 [81.0%]	56 [70.9%]	1,820 [95.5%]
CHALLENGER WINNERS				
≤4.99%	7 [0.4%]	22 [8.7%]	11 [13.9%]	40 [2.1%]
5%–9.99%	8 [0.5%]	13 [5.2%]	9 [11.4%]	30 [1.6%]
≥10%	0 [0.0%]	13 [5.2%]	3 [3.8%]	16 [0.8%]
Subtotal	15 [0.9%]	48 [19.0%]	23 [29.1%]	86 [4.5%]
TOTALS				
	1,575 [82.6%]	252 [13.2%]	79 [4.1%]	1,906[a] [100%]

Source: Compiled from data provided by the Federal Election Commission and the Clerk of the House.

[a]There were 264 open seat races and 5 incumbent vs. incumbent races, which, when added to the 1,906 races presented here, account for all 2,175 races that took place between 1992 and 2000.

victory decreases. These numbers are persuasive evidence that there is too little money rather than too much in our political process.

Whether money or partisan redistricting is most important in House races may seem unclear. But the empirical evidence strongly suggests that money, in sufficient quantities and effectively applied, is probably the dominant force in many if not most cases.

But it is undeniable that gerrymandering is also critically important. In fact, with the advent of high-tech computer modeling, redistricting has become so precise and refined that it is virtually certain that some significant number of House incumbents are in effect selecting constituents they will represent rather than the other way around.

Whatever the number, it is also virtually certain that in a significant number of congressional districts, the lack of competition in the general election has increased the importance of primary elections. Given that voter turnout is substantially lower in primaries (only about 17 percent of eligible voters turned out to vote in primaries in 2002),[3] personal wealth most certainly has a substantial impact on the outcome of many contested primaries because as voter turnout decreases, the importance of money spent on voter targeting and voter turnout drastically increases.

In any case it is clear that the combined effect of highly sophisticated gerrymandering techniques and court-sanctioned contribution limits has been to effectively transform America from a free democracy to a "managed" democracy controlled by a small elite. This observation is reinforced by the general election results for the U.S. House of Representatives in 2004. On December 10, 2004, the *Washington Post* reported the following:

> House members running for reelection this year widened their fundraising advantage over challengers, part of the reason 98 percent of them were able to hold on to their offices, according to a new study. The average amount raised by incumbents was up 20 percent over that of the previous election, while the fundraising by opponents declined by 6 percent on average, according to the Campaign Finance Institute, a Washington-based research group.
>
> "Political competition, the lifeblood of democracy, is under siege," Steve Weissman, a spokesman for the institute, said in a statement released with the study. Of the 401 House members who sought reelection in 399 contests last month, 394 will return to Washington next month. Two of those who lost faced other incumbents after their congressional districts were redrawn based on the 2000 census. In 36 districts, there was no incumbent. The officeholders raised, on average, $1.1 million, while challengers took in an average of $321,979.

FUND-RAISING RATIOS–HOUSE

Table 12.5 is a summary by source of all the money raised by House candidates for the period 1992–2000. (A further breakdown of these data can be found at www.moneypowerandelections.org.) The fund-raising ratios listed below are derived from the data in this table. These ratios highlight the financial advantage winning candidates, mostly incumbents, enjoy over losing candidates, who are mostly nonwealthy challengers.

House Incumbents Reelected (1992–2000)

- The average total amount raised by the 1,820 winning incumbents was $654,206, compared with $227,889 raised by their challengers, a 2.9 to 1 advantage for the incumbents.

Table 12.5. Sources of funding for House candidates, 1992–2000

	No. of candidates	Candidate contribution	PACs and party	Individuals	Total
	ELECTIONS WON BY INCUMBENTS				
Winning incumbents					
Totals	1,820	$18,241,955	$542,590,153	$629,823,310	$1,190,655,418
Avg. per candidate		$10,023	$298,126	$346,057	$654,206
% by category		2%	46%	53%	100%
Losing challengers					
Totals	1,374[a]	$69,814,200	$60,083,792	$183,220,899	$313,118,891
Avg. per candidate		$50,811	$43,729	$133,349	$227,889
% by category		22%	19%	59%	100%
	ELECTIONS WON BY CHALLENGERS				
Winning challengers					
Totals	86	$9,147,331	$16,651,495	$45,996,770	$71,795,596
Avg. per candidate		$106,364	$193,622	$534,846	$834,833
% by category		13%	23%	64%	100%
Losing incumbents					
Totals	86	$2,232,600	$38,120,153	$47,578,969	$87,931,722
Avg. per candidate		$25,960	$443,258	$553,244	$1,022,462
% by category		3%	43%	54%	100%
	ELECTIONS FOR OPEN SEATS				
Winners					
Totals	264	$30,629,498	$59,837,722	$111,204,327	$201,671,547
Avg. per candidate		$116,021	$226,658	$421,229	$763,907
% by category		15%	30%	55%	100%
Losers					
Totals	254[b]	$31,855,946	$33,651,708	$65,569,087	$131,076,741
Avg. per candidate		$125,417	$132,487	$258,146	$516,050
% by category		24%	26%	50%	100%
	ELECTIONS FOR REDISTRICTED SEATS (incumbents vs. incumbents)				
Winners					
Totals	5	$185,934	$1,484,400	$2,292,360	$3,962,694
Avg. per candidate		$37,187	$296,880	$458,472	$792,539
% by category		5%	37%	58%	100%
Losers					
Totals	5	$66,500	$2,029,443	$1,875,734	$3,971,677
Avg. per candidate		$13,300	$405,889	$375,147	$794,335
% by category		2%	51%	47%	100%

Source: Compiled from data provided by the Federal Election Commission and the Clerk of the House.

Note: A further breakdown of these data may be found at www.moneypowerandelections.org.

[a]There were 446 incumbents with no financial opposition.

[b]There were ten open-seat winners with no financial opposition.

- The average amount raised from individuals by winning incumbents was $346,057, compared with $133,349 by their challengers, a 2.6 to 1 advantage for the incumbents.

- The average PAC and party fund-raising by winning incumbents was $298,126, compared with $43,729 by challengers, a 6.8 to 1 advantage for the incumbents.

- The average amount of personal money spent by losing challengers was $50,811, compared with $10,023 spent by winning incumbents. These challengers spent more than five times as much of their own money as did the winning incumbents.

House Incumbents Defeated (1992–2000)

- The average total amount raised by the eighty-six incumbents who were defeated was $1,022,462, and winning challengers raised $834,833, a 1.2 to 1 ratio. (The fact that the average losing incumbent raised more money than the average winning challenger strongly suggests the presence of additional resources being spent by outside forces, such as political party committees and special interest groups, on behalf of winning challengers.)

- The average amount raised from individuals by losing incumbents was $553,244, compared with $534,846 by winning challengers, a ratio of roughly 1 to 1.

- The average PAC and party fund-raising by incumbents was $443,258, compared with $193,622 by challengers, a 2.3 to 1 advantage for these incumbents, despite their defeat at the polls.

- The average amount of personal money spent by winning challengers was $106,364, or 4.1 times as much as the $25,960 losing incumbents spent on average, further evidence that it takes a commitment of personal wealth to defeat an incumbent.

House Open Seats (1992–2000)

- The average total amount raised by winners in open-seat races was $763,907, compared with $516,050 raised by losers, a 1.5 to 1 advantage.

- The average amount raised from individuals by winners was $421,229, compared with $258,146 raised by losers, a 1.6 to 1 advantage.

- The average PAC and party fund-raising by winners was $226,658, compared with $132,487 by losers, a 1.7 to 1 advantage.

- The average amount of personal money spent by losers was $125,417, compared with $116,021 spent by winners, a 1.1 to 1 ratio.

House Incumbents Defeating Incumbents (1990–2000 Redistricting)

- The average total amount raised by incumbents defeating other incumbents in redistricting races was $792,539, compared with $794,335 raised by incumbents who lost to other incumbents in such races, a ratio of roughly 1 to 1.

- The average PAC and party fund-raising by incumbent losers was $405,889, compared with $296,880 by winners, a 1.4 to 1 ratio. (PACs as a group gave on average $100,000 more to losing incumbents pitted against other incumbents. This irregularity is an indication of the strong "protective" instincts within the PAC community for favored incumbents. It probably also reflects the fund-raising effectiveness of a desperate incumbent caught up in a tight race.)

FUND-RAISING RATIOS–SENATE

Table 12.6 is a summary by source of all the money raised by Senate candidates for the period 1992–2000. (A further breakdown of these data can be found at www.moneypowerandelections.org.) The fund-raising ratios listed below are derived from the data in this table. Again, these ratios highlight the financial advantage of winning candidates, who, in the Senate, include a somewhat larger proportion of wealthy challengers than in the House, along with, of course, a preponderance of incumbents.

Senate Incumbents Reelected (1992–2000)

- The average total amount raised by the 114 winning incumbents was $3,681,792, compared with $1,974,772 raised by their challengers, a 1.9 to 1 advantage for the incumbents.

- The average amount raised from individuals by winning incumbents was $2,402,136, compared with $1,250,826 by challengers, a 1.9 to 1 advantage for the incumbents.

Table 12.6. Sources of funding for Senate candidates, 1992–2000

	No. of candidates	Candidate contribution	PACs and party	Individuals	Total
		ELECTIONS WON BY INCUMBENTS			
Winning incumbents					
Totals	114[a]	$27,403,627	$118,477,177	$273,843,520	$419,724,324
Avg. per candidate		$240,383	$1,039,273	$2,402,136	$3,681,792
% by category		7%	28%	65%	100%
Losing challengers					
Totals	113[a]	$61,824,014	$19,981,953	$141,343,322	$223,149,289
Avg. per candidate		$547,115	$176,831	$1,250,826	$1,974,772
% by category		28%	9%	63%	100%
		ELECTIONS WON BY CHALLENGERS			
Winning challengers					
Totals	15	$50,200,191	$9,716,202	$54,705,356	$114,621,749
Avg. per candidate		$3,346,679	$647,747	$3,647,024	$7,641,450
% by category		44%	8%	48%	100%
Losing incumbents					
Totals	15	$2,370,323	$25,017,370	$71,474,459	$98,862,152
Avg. per candidate		$158,022	$1,667,825	$4,764,964	$6,590,810
% by category		2%	25%	72%	100%
		ELECTIONS FOR OPEN SEATS			
Winners					
Totals	38	$77,980,767	$33,469,919	$109,929,590	$221,380,276
Avg. per candidate		$2,052,125	$880,787	$2,892,884	$5,825,797
% by category		35%	15%	50%	100%
Losers					
Totals	38	$15,052,958	$21,476,141	$102,675,348	$139,204,447
Avg. per candidate		$396,130	$565,162	$2,701,983	$3,663,275
% by category		11%	15%	74%	100%

Source: Compiled from data provided by the Federal Election Commission and the Clerk of the House.

Note: A further breakdown of these data may be found at www.moneypowerandelections.org.

[a] John Breaux (D-LA) ran unopposed in his 1992 Senate campaign.

- The average PAC and party fund-raising by winning incumbents was $1,039,273, compared with $176,831 by challengers, a 5.9 to 1 advantage for the incumbents.
- The average amount of personal money spent by losing challengers was $547,115, compared with $240,383 spent by winning incumbents, a 2.3 to 1 ratio.

Senate Incumbents Defeated (1992–2000)

- The average total amount raised by the fifteen challengers who defeated incumbents was $7,641,450, compared with $6,590,810 raised by losing incumbents, a 1.2 to 1 advantage.
- The average amount raised from individuals by losing incumbents was $4,764,964, compared with $3,647,024 by winning challengers, a 1.3 to 1 ratio.
- The average PAC and party fund-raising by losing incumbents was $1,667,825, compared with $647,747 by winning challengers, a 2.6 to 1 ratio.
- The average amount of personal money spent by winning challengers was $3,346,674, 21.2 times as much as the $158,022 losing incumbents spent on average.

Senate Open Seats (1992–2000)

- The average total amount raised by winners was $5,825,797, compared with $3,663,275 raised by losers, a 1.6 to 1 advantage.
- The average amount of personal money spent by winners was $2,052,125, compared with $396,130 by losers, 5.2 times as much.

527 GROUPS

There has been much discussion and confusion about 527 groups. Simply stated, any organization in America whose primary purpose is to accept contributions and make expenditures in an attempt to influence "the selection, nomination, election, or appointment of any individual to any Federal, State or local public office" qualifies under Section 527 of the IRS

Code for tax exemption of funds used for "exempt function purposes." Funds spent by these entities for anything else is subject to federal taxation at the highest corporate rate.

Section 527 came into existence as a result of the Watergate scandal. At the end of the 1972 presidential campaign, the Committee to Re-elect the President (CREEP) had over $2 million in the bank. The IRS wanted a chunk of this money. Thus the requirement that "exemption function income" be used exclusively for exemption function purposes originated. Monies used to fund illegal burglaries, hush money, and dirty tricks are not exempt function purposes. So by creating Section 527 the IRS was able to collect a lot of money from CREEP.

What confuses the issue regarding 527 groups is the Supreme Court's *Buckley v. Valeo* decision. The Founding Fathers' purpose in establishing the Bill of Rights was to put certain liberties beyond the reach of government interference. As Chief Justice John Marshall stated in his famous *Marbury v. Madison* decision establishing the theoretical foundation of judicial review, "The powers of the legislature are defined and limited; and that those limits may not be mistaken, or forgotten, the Constitution is written."[4] The First Amendment says that "Congress shall make no law . . . abridging the freedom of speech . . . ; or the right of the people peaceably to assemble, and to petition the Government." The campaign finance reform laws blatantly violate these prohibitions. The High Court knew it was logically impossible to honor the First Amendment while declaring campaign finance reform constitutional. They could do one or the other but not both. Unfortunately, they chose to ignore this irony. Instead, they pursued an illogical line of reasoning that gutted the First Amendment by allowing the government to encroach into an area specifically restricted by the Framers without at the same time effectively regulating campaign finance. The Supreme Court tried to evade this contradiction by using erudite but specious reasoning, but its artful distinctions have not worked. Instead, the Court gave us the worst of both worlds: If a political organization expressly advocates the election or defeat of a candidate, it does *not* have unlimited free speech and must abide by all the governmental limits and rules that Congress chooses to impose. But if an organization does not expressly advocate the election or defeat of a candidate, it *has* unlimited free speech and does not have to abide by any governmental limits or rules. Thus in *Buckley v. Valeo* the Supreme Court created two types of 527 groups: those that have unrestricted free speech and those that don't.

This absurd interpretation of the First Amendment in *Buckley v. Valeo* coupled with BCRA's elimination of soft-money contributions to national party committees (i.e., contributions of any amount from corporations or unions and contributions from individuals above federal limits) have encouraged the emergence of the now notorious sort of 527 groups whose smear tactics made headlines throughout the 2004 election cycle. This rise in the importance of these fringe organizations that seem to thrive on attack ads has exposed the absurdity of campaign finance reform and the Supreme Court's decisions. Prior to BCRA, party committees dominated the process. Now the action has shifted to renegade 527 groups because they are the last outposts where citizens can congregate to exercise their right of free speech. To this extent their existence is to be welcomed.

The purpose of 527 groups like Swift Boat Veterans for Truth, MoveOn.org, Americans Coming Together, Club for Growth, and a host of other, less-well-known groups is to actively pursue the spirit of the First Amendment while only barely abiding by the letter of the law. Unfortunately such groups are like political pirates, answerable to no one. As a consequence, they have little incentive to be prudent in their words or actions. If necessary they can easily disband and reorganize under different names. They can meddle in the election process with all the flexibility of a con artist. And all too often, they do.

In reality the contribution limits imposed by campaign finance reform are simply a political form of government-mandated price controls. Like mandated economic price controls, they create unfair scarcity and black markets. In politics rogue 527 groups function like black markets. The existence of such groups is prima facie evidence that reformers, both on and off the Supreme Court, are failing at their larger aim of improving public confidence in politics and government. Like mandated economic price controls, mandated political price controls will never work.

If Congress and the High Court continue to aggressively expand their restrictions and limits, ordinary citizens will soon begin to realize they are losing their rights of free speech and free political association. Alternatively, if the government is unable to effectively enforce the High Court's twisted logic that is currently the law of the land, then the escalating evasion and political rancor that is sure to follow will breed further disrespect for the law, the Constitution, and our entire system of government. Either course weakens American democracy.

NATIONAL PARTY COMMITTEES

A reminder is perhaps in order about what is referred to as "hard" and "soft" money. Hard money consists of contributions raised in compliance with federal law and limits. Essentially, it is money raised from individuals up to the legal maximum. Soft money consists of donations of any amount from corporations and labor unions and donations from individuals above the prescribed federal limits. Table 12.7 shows the total hard and soft money raised by the three Republican and three Democrat national party committees combined for 2001–2002, the last election cycle prior to the enactment of BCRA. Soft money represented approximately 43 percent of the *net* dollars raised by Republicans and 57 percent of the *net* funds raised by Democrats. BCRA stripped away this soft-money component (a combined total of roughly $500 million gross or $450 million net) from the two major political parties.

Much of the soft money that once flowed to political parties has now been diverted to 527 groups. This is tragic. Over the years, political party

Table 12.7. Hard and soft money raised by Republican and Democratic national committees, 2001–2002

	Republican national committees	% of Republican total	Democratic national committees	% of Democratic total
HARD MONEY				
Gross receipts	$402,065,392	62%	$220,244,544	47%
Estimated fund-raising cost	$100,000,000	–	$55,000,000	–
Estimated net	$302,065,392	57%	$165,244,544	43%
SOFT MONEY				
Gross receipts	$250,032,620	38%	$245,850,711	53%
Estimated fund-raising cost	$25,000,000	–	$24,000,000	–
Estimated net	$225,032,020	43%	$221,850,711	57%
TOTAL				
Gross receipts	$652,098,012	100%	$466,095,255	100%
Estimated fund-raising cost	$125,000,000	–	$79,000,000	–
Estimated net	$527,098,002	100%	$387,095,255	100%

Source: Gross receipts provided by the Federal Election Commission, October 24, 2002. Estimated fund-raising costs are percentage estimates based upon the author's experience and exclude prospecting expenses.

committees have repeatedly demonstrated that they tend to use such monies, which they fully disclosed, much more responsibly than do renegade 527 groups. This is not to say party officials are less passionate about politics. The reason for their restraint is much more pragmatic. Political parties have to be more prudent because of the potential long-term consequences of their actions. In addition, parties have a responsibility to a broad field of candidates and constituents, who are quick to let party officials know when they've gone too far or are otherwise out of sync with the desires and objectives of the diverse groups they represent. Consequently, party committees tend to be more politically mainstream than the shadowy 527 groups.

Table 12.8 shows the approximate number of new donors within specific giving ranges each party would have to find in order to make up for the net loss in soft money mandated by BCRA. When these numbers are compared with the numbers of actual donors in recent years (see Table 15.1), we see the practical impossibility of either party recruiting enough new donors to make up for the net loss of soft money. Both political parties would literally have to double their existing donor bases. Absent the occurrence of some cataclysmic or otherwise significant event that dramatically changes the status quo, doubling the size of either party's donor base would be virtually impossible.

Table 12.8. Additional donors and contributions needed per party to replace soft-money donations

Giving range	Avg. contribution	No. of contributors	Gross	Cost factor[a]	Net
≥$10,000	$15,000	16,000	$240,000,000	5%	$228,000,000
$1,000–$9,999	$2,500	100,000	$250,000,000	10%	$225,000,000
$200–$999	$500	560,000	$280,000,000	20%	$224,000,000
<$200	$100	3,500,000	$350,000,000	35%	$227,500,000

[a]Estimated fund-raising cost excluding prospecting expenses.

In fact, the heightened level of fund-raising competition that is certain to occur within each political party as a result of the loss of soft-money revenue is more likely to *shrink* rather than expand either party's existing donor base. The internal fight for funds within both parties as they attempt to recover the lost soft-money revenue will almost certainly result in a smothering through oversolicitation of known donors. These geese that have traditionally supplied the golden eggs will become worn out and possibly alienated.

Tragically, the fund-raising pool for both political parties is simply too small and the financial restrictions too severe for all the candidates and party committees to prosper under the new law. Over time, both parties are likely to contract significantly. Many reformers have worried that some loophole might be discovered that would undermine their handiwork. On the contrary, the wolves of reform did their work well. There are no escape hatches or loopholes available to political party committees. And contrary to conventional wisdom, this is not good news for America.

A NATURAL OUTGROWTH OF DEMOCRACY

Under our system of government, political parties are crucial and unique entities. There is nothing else like them in our society. Though they are technically nonprofit organizations, they are unlike any others. Unlike most charitable or educational organizations, partisan political committees always have a political agenda based on a unique set of guiding principles. Party committees raise and spend funds to elect candidates who represent the general goals and ideals of the party and who will vote with the party. Political parties attempt to build coalitions of like-minded citizens. They are not established to do charitable work. Nor are they single-purpose special interest groups that focus on issues within some narrow sphere. They are focused exclusively on furthering specific political ends that generally conform to their broad guiding principles.

Political parties are a natural offshoot of democracy, an essential concomitant. They developed to promote certain ideas and interests, but they have also had the effect of curtailing the influence of unbridled wealth functioning autonomously. Prior to the passage of campaign finance reform, a political party could, by acting as a financial clearinghouse, attempt to match or even exceed the investment of a single rich person or a small group of zealots operating as a troublesome 527 entity. Those who might otherwise have been able to buy an election for themselves or for candidates who support their interests had to contend with a strong political party structure. The Framers instinctively understood this, which is why they did not attempt to inhibit or restrict political factions and did everything they could to encourage the rich, the not so rich, and the poor to commingle their resources through coalition groups and political entities that eventually evolved into parties.

Our nation owes a lot to our two-party political process. It has protected America from the curse of multiparty coalition government. The time has come for us to view our competitive two-party political process for what it is: one of the fundamental strengths of American democracy. Before it's too late, Congress and the courts need to stop playing Russian roulette with this important American institution that has served our country so well.

13 EMPIRICAL EVIDENCE

Sell not . . . liberty to purchase power.

Benjamin Franklin

Back in 1789, America's first Congress had 91 members—65 in the House and 26 in the Senate. Today there are 535 voting members of Congress: 435 in the House and 100 in the Senate, a 488 percent increase. In the intervening 216 years 11,743 individuals have had the honor to serve in the halls of Congress.

CHANGE IN YEARS OF SERVICE

House

From 1789 through 1920, a total of 7,245 individuals were elected to serve in the House (69 percent of the total number to the present day) for an average of 2.1 terms, or just over four years. Compare this "citizen legislature" turnover rate to the projected average tenure of the House member in the 107th Congress elected in 2000, which is almost eight terms.

Table 13.1. House members and senators in 107th Congress by decade elected

Decade elected	No. of House members	No. of senators
1950s	1	3
1960s	8	3
1970s	50	16
1980s	99	25
1990s	277	53

Source: Compiled from data provided by the Clerk of the House.

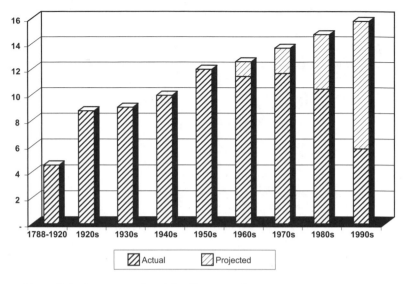

Figure 13.1. Average term length for House members
Data provided by the Clerk of the House

Table 13.1 shows the number of representatives and senators currently serving who were elected in each decade since the 1950s. Figure 13.1 shows the average length of tenure of House members first elected in each decade since the 1920s along with the overall average from 1789 to 1920. As Figure 13.1 shows, the average length of service in the House has skyrocketed to a projected average of more than fourteen years for representatives first elected to the House in the 1990s, assuming the trend over the last eighty years continues.

Senate

From 1789 through 1913, when the Seventeenth Amendment was ratified, members of Senate were appointed by their respective state legislatures. In 1920 the Nineteenth Amendment was ratified, giving women the right to vote. These two constitutional changes marked the beginning of the modern political era. In the eighty-year period ending with the election of the 107th Congress in 2000, 692 individuals served in the U.S. Senate. Table 13.1 shows the number of senators currently serving who were elected in each decade since the 1950s. Figure 13.2 graphically illustrates how the average tenure in the Senate has increased from just under eight years in

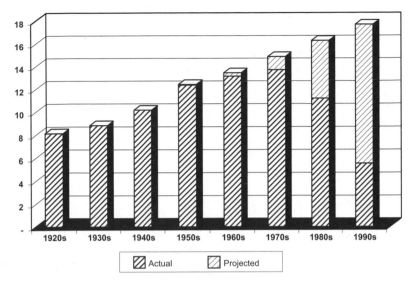

Figure 13.2. Average term length for Senate members
Data provided by the Clerk of the House

1920 to almost eighteen years in the 1990s, assuming the trend of the last eighty years continues.

INCUMBENTS' REELECTION RATES– HOUSE AND SENATE

Table 13.2 shows the incumbent reelection rates for both the House and Senate for each election cycle from 1920 to 2000. (More detailed data can be found at www.moneypowerandelections.org.) Figures 13.3 and 13.4 are graphs of these rates.

The reelection rate for both chambers of Congress is high, but the re-election rate for the House is notably higher. One reason for this difference is the fact that individuals are typically appointed to fill Senate vacancies prior to a general or special election. In calculating the reelection statistics, these appointed senators are counted as incumbents, and the data reflect the fact that appointed senators are more likely to be defeated than their previously elected counterparts. Conversely, House vacancies are filled only by special election; there are no appointees running as incumbents who might be more vulnerable to defeat.

Table 13.2. House and Senate reelection rates, 1920–2000

Election cycle	House reelection rate (%)[a]	Senate reelection rate (%)[b]	Election cycle	House reelection rate (%)[a]	Senate reelection rate (%)[b]
1920–21	86.0	72.0	1962	94.6	85.3
1922–23	82.2	60.0	1964	88.4	87.5
1924–25	92.2	84.0	1966	89.8	96.7
1926	95.9	71.0	1968	97.8	83.3
1928	91.6	83.9	1970	96.9	80.0
1930–31	88.4	69.2	1972	96.0	80.8
1932–33	76.2	71.4	1974–75	89.8	88.5
1934	89.0	75.0	1976	96.6	64.0
1936–37	91.6	81.5	1978	95.0	68.2
1938	82.6	82.1	1980	91.6	64.0
1940–41	90.7	88.9	1982–83	92.4	93.5
1942	87.5	75.0	1984	96.1	89.7
1944	91.0	84.0	1986	98.5	75.0
1946–47	87.0	70.8	1988	98.3	88.5
1948–49	82.6	62.5	1990–91	96.3	97.0
1950	91.7	80.8	1992–93	93.1	82.1
1952	93.6	66.7	1994	91.1	92.3
1954	94.8	80.0	1996	94.5	95.0
1956–57	96.3	86.2	1998	98.5	89.7
1958–59	90.8	64.3	2000	98.5	79.3
1960–61	94.0	93.5	Average	92.0	80.3

Source: Compiled from data provided by the Clerk of the House.

Note: Further House and Senate reelection data may be found at www.moneypowerandelections.org.

[a]Includes only general elections.

[b]Includes all general and special elections.

IMPACT OF *BUCKLEY V. VALEO* ON FEDERAL ELECTIONS

The various tables and graphs in this chapter demonstrate that the campaign finance restrictions imposed by Congress and constitutionalized by the High Court have been counterproductive, empowering the rich and reducing the competitiveness of the political arena. In the *Buckley v. Valeo* decision, the Supreme Court stated that the "contribution provisions" in

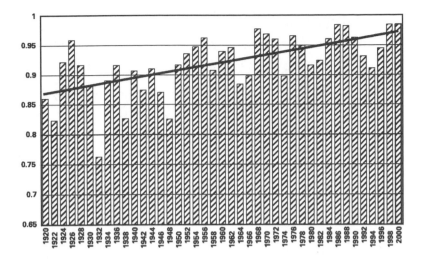

Figure 13.3. House reelection rates, 1788–2000
Data provided by the Clerk of the House

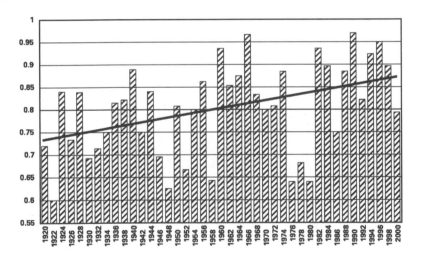

Figure 13.4. Senate reelection rates, 1788–2000
Data provided by the Clerk of the House

the Federal Election Campaign Acts of 1971 and 1974 "serve the basic governmental interest . . .without directly impinging upon the rights of individual citizens and candidates to engage in political debate and discussion. . . ."[1] The High Court could not have been more wrong. Its decisions have silenced nonwealthy challengers, enabling even more incumbent and wealthy candidates to win and to win with larger victory margins.

House Reelection Results

Table 13.3 and Figure 13.5 show the election rates for House incumbents and challengers for the whole country, the old Confederacy (eleven southern states), and the balance of the country without the South. Given that the states of the old Confederacy emerged from Reconstruction as a rock-solid single-party voting bloc in Congress and generally remained one until the latter part of the twentieth century, Tables 13.5 and 13.8 and Figures 13.7 and 13.10 exclude those eleven southern States.

While *Buckley v. Valeo* also had a repressive impact on elections in the South, the impact is not as obviously dramatic, given the longtime domination of a single party in the region. As a consequence, both the election results and victory margin for the southern states are shown separately in Figures 13.5 and 13.6 and Tables 13.3 and 13.4. This separation gives a more realistic idea of the devastating impact of *Buckley v. Valeo* on the rest of the country.

For the period 1976–2000, the reelection rate for House incumbents outside the South was 95.4 percent. In the same period, the chances of a

Table 13.3. House incumbents' and challengers' winning percentages with and without the South, pre- and post-Buckley

	Incumbents	Challengers
U.S.A.		
Pre-Buckley (1920–1974)	90.6%	9.4%
Post-Buckley (1975–2000)	95.7%	4.3%
SOUTH		
Pre-Buckley (1920–1974)	98.0%	2.0%
Post-Buckley (1975–2000)	96.5%	3.5%
U.S. WITHOUT SOUTH		
Pre-Buckley (1920–1974)	88.3%	11.7%
Post-Buckley (1975–2000)	95.4%	4.6%
Change	7.1	(7.1)
Percent increase (decrease)	8%	(60.7%)

Source: Compiled from data provided by the Clerk of the House.

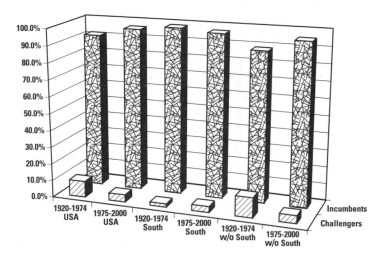

Figure 13.5. Winning percentage of House incumbents and challengers with and without the South, pre- and post-Buckley

Data provided by the Clerk of the House

challenger defeating an incumbent outside the South fell from 11.7 percent to 4.6 percent, an unbelievable 60.7 percent drop (see Table 13.3). The margin of victory for House incumbents outside the South (Table 13.5 and Figure 13.7) also generally increased over the same period, as the number of extremely competitive House races dropped by 42.9 percent, the number of competitive races dropped by 47.1 percent, the number of semicompetitive races dropped by 39.8 percent the number of noncompetitive races dropped by 39.3 percent, and the no-contest races (those with a margin of victory of 15 percent or more) shot up by a remarkable 25.4 percent. Given that these dramatic changes correspond so closely with the changes in the law, these results cannot simply be brushed aside as an aberration.

Senate Reelection Results

The impact of *Buckley v. Valeo* on the Senate has been very much the same as on House elections. The Senate incumbent reelection percentage outside the South increased by 12.2 percent, while the percentage of challengers winning dropped by 35.8 percent for the period 1976–2000 (see Table 13.6 and Figure 13.8). In the same period the number of Senate incumbents winning reelection by victory margins of 15 percent or more increased

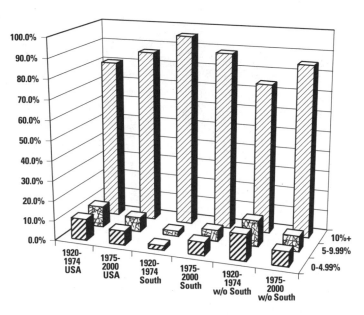

Figure 13.6. Change in margin of victory in House races by competitiveness category, pre- and post-Buckley

Data provided by the Clerk of the House

Table 13.4. House races by margin of victory percentage with and without the South, pre- and post-Buckley

	MARGIN OF VICTORY		
	≥10%	5%–9.99%	≤4.99%
U.S.A.			
Pre-Buckley (1920–1974)	79.2%	10.3%	10.5%
Post-Buckley (1975–2000)	85.8%	7.1%	7.1%
SOUTH			
Pre-Buckley (1920–1974)	95.1%	2.6%	2.3%
Post-Buckley (1975–2000)	87.9%	5.5%	6.6%
U.S. WITHOUT SOUTH			
Pre-Buckley (1920–1974)	74.1%	12.8%	13.1%
Post-Buckley (1975–2000)	85.0%	7.7%	7.3%
Change	10.9	(5.1)	(5.8)
Percent increase (decrease)	14.7%	(39.8%)	(44.3%)

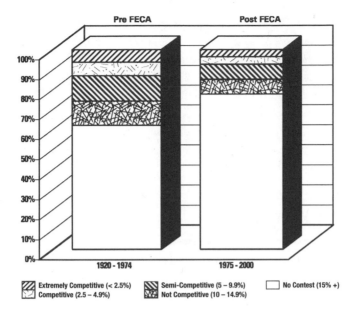

Figure 13.7. Competitiveness of House elections, pre- and post-Buckley
Data provided by the Clerk of the House

Table 13.5. Change in margin of victory in House races by competitiveness category, pre- and post-Buckley without the South

	Pre-Buckley (1920–1974)	Post-Buckley (1975–2000)	Change	% increase (decrease)
Extremely competitive (≤2.5%)	6.3%	3.6%	(2.7)	(42.9%)
Competitive (2.5%–4.9%)	6.8%	3.6%	(3.2)	(47.1%)
Semicompetitive (5%–9.9%)	12.8%	7.7%	(5.1)	(39.8%)
Not competitive (10%–14.9%)	12.2%	7.4%	(4.8)	(39.3%)
No contest (≥15%)	61.9%	77.6%	15.7	25.4%

Source: Compiled from data provided by the Clerk of the House.

by 32 percent (see Tables 13.7 and 13.8 and Figures 13.9 and 13.10). The number of extremely competitive Senate races dropped by 18.8 percent, the number of competitive Senate races dropped by 20.5 percent, the number of semicompetitive Senate races dropped by 32.5 percent, and the number of noncompetitive Senate races dropped by 12.7 percent during the same period.

Clearly, *Buckley v. Valeo* has stifled the competitiveness of Senate and House elections. And the High Court's declaring the Bipartisan Campaign

Reform Act (BCRA) constitutional will only make things worse. This assessment is reinforced by a June 27, 2003, news release from the Center for Responsive Politics, which found that 94 percent of winning congressional candidates outspent their losing opponents.[2] In addition, as Steven Hill and Rob Richie point out in their July 1, 2003, *Washington Post* editorial, only four House challengers defeated incumbents in 2002, "the fewest in history." It would not be surprising if, in the not-too-distant future, the reelection rate for incumbents reached nearly 100 percent. Is this democracy or the pretense of democracy?

PRESIDENTIAL CAMPAIGNS

Campaign finance reform has essentially made presidential campaigns much less national in scope. This contraction in range is caused by conditions imposed by public financing. During a presidential election, candidates may receive public dollars if they agree to abide by certain spending limitations. During the primary this limit is approximately 25 percent of the following arbitrary formula: sixteen cents times the voting-age population, adjusted for inflation since 1976. During the general election the spending limit is about 50 percent of this formula.

Table 13.6. Senate incumbents' and challengers' winning percentages with and without the South, pre- and post-Buckley

	Incumbents	Challengers
U.S.A.		
Pre-Buckley (1920–1974)	79.8%	20.2%
Post-Buckley (1975–2000)	84.0%	16.0%
SOUTH		
Pre-Buckley (1920–1974)	98.1%	1.9%
Post-Buckley (1975–2000)	84.9%	15.1%
U.S. WITHOUT SOUTH		
Pre-Buckley (1920–1974)	74.6%	25.4%
Post-Buckley (1975–2000)	83.7%	16.3%
Change	9.1	(9.1)
Percent increase (decrease)	12.2%	(35.8%)

Source: Compiled from data provided by the Clerk of the House.

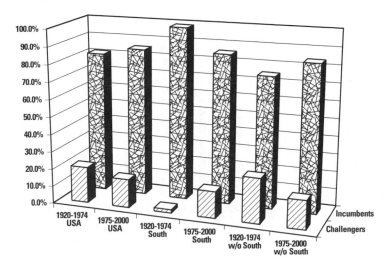

Figure 13.8. Winning percentage of Senate incumbents and challengers with and without the South, pre- and post-Buckley

Data provided by the Clerk of the House

Sound complicated? It is. The harsh fund-raising restrictions make it nearly impossible for candidates to raise more money for the general election campaign than they could receive through public financing. And once candidates accept public financing, they lack the dollars necessary to run a national campaign. As a result, they must use their limited financial resources to target certain swing states, which become the focus of presidential contests. This produces the unhealthy result of a few states being deluged by campaign advertising and candidate visits while most of the other states barely receive any attention from the candidates at all. By targeting only those swing states with the most electoral votes that are not firmly wedded to one candidate or the other, presidential campaigns have ceased to be national races. The only thing that makes them national in scope is the huge amount of free media exposure they receive.

This forced contraction of presidential campaigns means that every presidential candidate, including those who win, is forced to ignore sections of the country. This is bad for our country and bad for our democracy because only presidents who have established a presence and credible strength in all parts of the country truly have the electoral mandate to speak for the people of the United States.

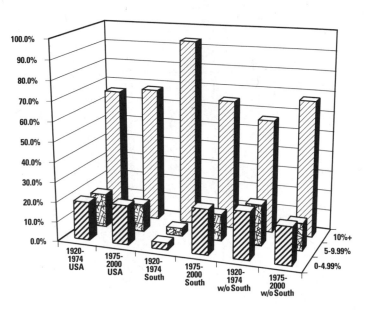

Figure 13.9. Change in margin of victory in Senate races by competitiveness category, pre- and post-Buckley

Data provided by the Clerk of the House

Table 13.7. Senate races by margin of victory percentage with and without the South, pre- and post-Buckley

	MARGIN OF VICTORY		
	≥10%	5%–9.99%	≤4.99%
	U.S.A.		
Pre-Buckley (1920–1974)	64.5%	16.6%	18.9%
Post-Buckley (1975–2000)	66.8%	13.6%	19.6%
	SOUTH		
Pre-Buckley (1920–1974)	92.8%	3.8%	3.4%
Post-Buckley (1975–2000)	64.3%	13.3%	22.4%
	U.S. WITHOUT SOUTH		
Pre-Buckley (1920–1974)	56.2%	20.3%	23.5%
Post-Buckley (1975–2000)	67.5%	13.7%	18.8%
Change	11.3	(6.6)	(4.7)
Percent increase (decrease)	20.1%	(32.5%)	(20%)

Source: Compiled from data provided by the Clerk of the House.

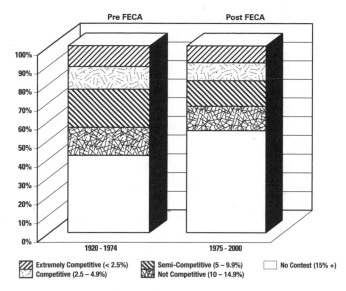

Figure 13.10. Competitiveness of Senate elections, pre- and post-Buckley
Data provided by the Clerk of the House

Table 13.8. Change in margin of victory in Senate races by competitiveness category, pre- and post-Buckley without the South

	Pre-Buckley (1920–1974)	Post-Buckley (1975–2000)	Change	Percent increase (decrease)
Extremely competitive (≤2.5%)	11.2%	9.1%	(2.1)	(18.8%)
Competitive (2.5%–4.9%)	12.2%	9.7%	(2.5)	(20.5%)
Semicompetitive (5%–9.9%)	20.3%	13.7%	(6.6)	(32.5%)
Not competitive (10%–14.9%)	15.0%	13.1%	(1.9)	(12.7%)
No contest (≥15%)	41.2%	54.4%	13.2	32.0%

Source: Compiled from data provided by the Clerk of the House.

Throughout American history, there has been concern among party leaders that their presidential nominee not be stigmatized as rigidly regional. Even in the period before the Civil War when the Democratic Party was dominant in the South, the opposition Whigs did not dare write off Dixie. They regularly gave their nomination to southerners or border-state politicians. The Democrats, for their part, went so far as to nominate a New Englander, Franklin Pierce, in 1852, in the hope of gaining northern votes.

Since the beginning of our republic, political leaders have attempted to unify all sections of America. Unfortunately, campaign finance reform has disdainfully brushed aside this striving for unity and replaced it with the polarization of presidential politics into two opposing partisan blocs of "red" and "blue" states. As more party identification colors start being added to this divisive concoction masquerading as "reform," we could begin to see presidential contests being decided in the House (which hasn't happened since 1824), and this of course would only fuel the fires of distrust and cynicism now permeating the electorate.

ELECTION COMPARISON: PRESIDENT, SENATE, HOUSE

Americans have traditionally focused most of their political attention on presidential power and presidential politics. Most people assume that congressional power and congressional elections are very similar to those of the presidency, but in fact they are quite different. One important difference is the relative competitiveness of presidential and congressional races. Table 13. 9 and Figure 13.11 provide a quantitative comparison of the margins of victory in presidential, Senate, and House races for the period 1920–2000. As the table and figure show, 47.7 percent of all presidential campaigns during this period were noncompetitive (victory margins of 10 percent or more), 28.6 percent were semicompetitive (victory margins of 5.0 to 9.9 percent), and 23.7 percent were competitive (victory margins

Table 13.9. Competitiveness of presidential, Senate, and House races, 1920–2000

	Noncompetitive (victory margin ≥10%)	Semicompetitive (victory margin 5%–9.9%)	Competitive (victory margin ≤4.9%)
Presidential races	47.7%	28.6%	23.7%
Senate races	65.3%	15.7%	19.0%
Difference between presidential and Senate races	17.6	(12.9)	(4.7)
Difference between presidential and Senate races (%)	36.9%	45.1%	(19.8%)
House races	81.3%	9.3%	9.4%
Difference between presidential and House races	33.6	(19.3)	(14.3)
Difference between presidential and House races (%)	70.4%	(67.5%)	(60.3%)

Source: Compiled from data provided by the Clerk of the House.

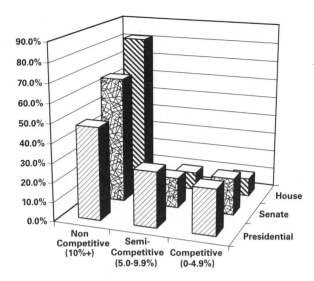

Figure 13.11. Competitiveness of presidential, Senate, and House races, 1920–2000
Data provided by the Clerk of the House

of 4.9 percent or less). Over the same period, Senate campaigns were less competitive than presidential campaigns, with 65.3 percent being noncompetitive and only 19.0 percent being competitive. House campaigns were the least competitive, with an astonishing 81.3 percent being noncompetitive and a mere 9.4 percent being competitive.

While Senate contests are not as competitive as presidential elections, they are still more competitive than races for the House. Senate candidates tend to spend larger amounts of personal wealth, especially Senate challengers. House challengers, on the other hand, seldom have adequate funding. As a consequence, they rarely run competitive races unless, of course, a challenger has the ability and the will to spend large amounts of personal wealth.

THE WASHINGTONIAN YARDSTICK:
A REASONABLE AMOUNT OF CAMPAIGN FUNDING

In July of 1758, running as a challenger, George Washington spent about $195 to win election to the Virginia House of Burgesses.[3] With 794 votes cast in the election, Washington spent roughly twenty-five cents per vote cast in his first successful campaign for office. That twenty-five cents adjusted for inflation would have been worth about $2.40 in 2000 dollars.[4]

Table 13.10 provides a summary of spending in all federal elections during the 1999–2000 election cycle in comparison with Washington's campaign spending, adjusted for inflation. Assuming it can be agreed that George Washington was an honest and virtuous man, then it would seem reasonable to use what he spent per vote cast to get elected to office in 1758 as a frame of reference to judge the legitimacy of modern-day political spending. As the table indicates, the total spent by all candidates and party committees at the federal level during the 1999–2000 election cycle is only 65 percent of what would have been spent if the standard set by the father of our country had been followed. So the idea that too much money is being spent on politics in America is another erroneous perception, if the standard set by George Washington is used as the framework of our analysis.

Table 13.10. Campaign spending in 2000 compared with George Washington's in 1758, adjusted for inflation

Category	No. of votes cast in 2000	Projected spending based on Washington's campaign[a]	Actual spending in 2000	% of Washington-based projection
Presidential	105,405,100	$505,945,000	$135,000,000	27%
Congressional	97,228,616	$466,695,000	$368,600,000	79%
Senate	79,315,481	$380,715,000	$244,800,000	64%
Subtotal	281,949,197	$1,353,355,000	$733,400,000	55%
Party	281,949,197	$1,353,355,000	$1,018,193,000	75%
Total		$2,706,710,000	$1,751,593,000	65%

Source: Number of votes and actual spending compiled from data provided by the Federal Election Commission.

[a]Assumes $2.40 spent by each of two candidates for each vote cast.

14 FREEDOM OF THE PRESS

> Without freedom of thought there can be no such thing as wisdom; and
> no such thing as public liberty, without freedom of speech.
>
> Benjamin Franklin

As we have seen, in crafting the First Amendment to the United States Constitution, the Framers made it crystal clear that Congress "shall make no law" restricting or interfering with four basic liberties: freedom of religion, freedom of speech, freedom of the press, and freedom of assembly.

Each of these rights had begun to take root just prior to the Pilgrims' disembarking at Plymouth, Massachusetts, on December 26, 1620. Before even setting foot in the new world, the Pilgrims created the first important document underpinning American democracy as we know it. Called the Mayflower Compact, it arose out of a need to maintain social and civic order in the New World. At its most basic, the Compact asserted and affirmed the Pilgrims' liberty and established the democratic concept that "just and equall lawes" would be enacted by the consent of the people. In its day, the Mayflower Compact was every bit as original and revolutionary as those later documents it helped to inspire, the Declaration of Independence, the Constitution, and the Bill of Rights.

Over the next 150 years, each colony experimented in its own way with various aspects of sprouting self-government, albeit within the framework of the British monarchy. And, as we know, after the American Revolution had freed the colonies from the king, each became sovereign over itself.

However, as separate and independent units, the colonies realized they were weak and vulnerable. That's why they willingly worked together wrestling with the tribulations and dangers of establishing a new form of centralized government. Yet as important as it was "to form a more perfect union," none of the colonies were willing to enter into any new arrangement that did not protect their hard-won freedoms, including these four unalienable liberties. Indeed, the Federalist Papers were written to reassure the Anti-Federalists and the people that such freedoms would be protected.

Experience had taught all thirteen colonies what the Pilgrims considered an article of faith generations before: namely, the uncompromising importance of freedom in the New World. In *The Basic Symbols of the American Tradition,* Willmoore Kendall and George Carey see the compact as laying the groundwork for the future development of an American polity based on freedom.[1] To be sure, the freedoms specified in the First Amendment are not explicitly commended in the Mayflower Compact, but they are there in potentia and for this reason can be viewed as symbolically representing the fulfillment of the "Pilgrims' promise" stated in the Mayflower Compact. Their protection was not negotiable. This is why, together, they became the foundation of the First Amendment.

My reason for reiterating this bit of history at the beginning of this chapter is to set the stage for discussing yet another sacred right that has thus far been largely ignored. That is, of course, the freedom of the press.

Given the clear and unmistakable protection of free speech afforded to the press by the First Amendment, it is puzzling that the Federal Election Campaign Act of 1974 includes the following language:

SEC.100.73 NEWS STORY, COMMENTARY, OR EDITORIAL BY THE MEDIA.

Any cost incurred in covering or carrying a news story, commentary, or editorial by any broadcasting station (including a cable television operator, programmer or producer), newspaper, magazine, or other periodical publication is not a contribution unless the facility is owned or controlled by any political party, political committee, or candidate, in which case the costs for a news story:

(a) That represents a bona fide news account communicated in a publication of general circulation or on a licensed broadcasting facility; and

(b) That is part of a general pattern of campaign-related news accounts that give reasonably equal coverage to all opposing candidates in the circulation or listening area, is not a contribution.

Similarly, the Bipartisan Campaign Reform Act of 2002 includes the following:

SEC.201 DISCLOSURE OF ELECTIONEERING COMMUNICATIONS.

(B) EXCEPTIONS.—The term 'electioneering communications' does not include—

(i) a communication appearing in a news story, commentary, or editorial distributed through the facilities of any broadcasting station, unless such facilities are owned or controlled by any political party, political committee, or candidate. . . .

The obvious question these exemptions raise is, why was this verbiage considered necessary? At first blush we might be pleased that the reformers saw fit to continue to recognize the press's sacred right of free political speech, especially when we see what their legislation has done with the right of ordinary citizens to free speech. However, the unrestricted voice of the press in all aspects of the election process should not require any additional guarantees outside the Constitution. Therefore the mere existence of these paragraphs concerning the press should be troubling to anyone who cares about freedom of speech in America. Inclusion of these special exemptions in campaign finance reform legislation only makes sense if they are viewed as loopholes in that legislation. Their very presence suggests a conscious, or perhaps unconscious, acknowledgment that free speech was being abridged somewhere in these laws.

Three possible reasons the reformers might have felt the need to insert these press exemptions into their legislation suggest themselves:

1. If the advocates of campaign finance reform were aware that their legislation trampled on the First Amendment, they might have wanted to exempt the press. Aware that most editors, reporters, and commentators were favorable to their cause, they certainly did not want to risk alienating a strong ally.

2. Fully expecting that their legislation would be challenged in court, the reformers might have reasoned that their chances of surviving a court battle would be enhanced if the press were specifically exempted. Such a maneuver could improve the likelihood that their attack on one of America's four fundamental freedoms might slip through.

3. As a powerful special interest group itself, the press might have understood early in the debate that the ever-expanding tentacles of campaign finance reform could one day encircle them. To guard

against this possibility, they may have used their considerable lobbying prowess. Protecting one's own self-interest is a compelling motivation.

But whatever the reason for the existence of these special Press exemptions, it is not good news.

By including the First Amendment in the Bill of Rights, the Founding Fathers hoped to create an impenetrable barrier that protected the press as well as every citizen's right to free, unrestrained political speech. In its *Buckley v. Valeo* and BCRA decisions the Supreme Court has converted that impenetrable barrier into little more than a minor speed bump by allowing Congress jurisdiction over an unalienable right, free political speech, which was explicitly and unambiguously forbidden by the Founding Fathers in the First Amendment.

Thus the High Court's action has substantially broadened Congress's authority in the area of free speech. Given that the Court's decision also implicitly sanctioned the special language insert in campaign finance reform exempting the Press, can it now be argued that the press's right to free speech is no longer a constitutional right but rather only a legislative right? In other words, if a simple majority in Congress can *grant* the press a privileged status in the area of political expression, does it not also follow that that same simple majority can also *take* that privilege away? Is it possible that in their zeal for perfection, the reformers have unwittingly also weakened, or perhaps even eliminated, the press's constitutional right to free political expression?

When Congress passed the Alien and Sedition Acts in 1798, criminalizing written criticism of the government, a number of Jeffersonian newspaper publishers were convicted under the terms of the Sedition Act. During the Civil War, hundreds of northern newspaper editors and owners who criticized the administration were incarcerated. None was ever served a warrant, and some were held incommunicado in military prisons without ever receiving due process. If free speech is no longer viewed as an inalienable right by the courts, why should we trust them to view freedom of the press differently?

Freedom is a wonderful idea. Yet one only needs to read a few pages of Churchill's *History of the English-Speaking Peoples* to realize what a tender plant democracy really is and how desperately it needs to be safeguarded by the very same institutions within our society that have chosen instead to attack it relentlessly.

When our basic freedoms, which the Founders believed were God-given, not granted by government, are suddenly placed under the control of lawmakers and the courts, we are all in trouble. Regrettably, too many people in the press, Congress, and the courts have repeatedly demonstrated by their actions in the struggle over campaign finance reform that they have no fundamental understanding of what really makes our unique form of democracy work.

When it comes to trying to maintain a satisfactory equilibrium between the influence of money and power, there are no perfect solutions. There are only tradeoffs. People can demand square circles if they want, but that does not mean they will get them. What they are more likely to get is the illusion of a solution created by those seeking to satisfy their own self-interest. In truth, that is what we got with campaign finance reform: the illusion of a solution.

What most people in the press are reluctant to admit (or haven't particularly thought about) is that when the Supreme Court declared both campaign finance reform bills constitutional, it was not just incumbents and the wealthy who gained greater power at the expense of the nonwealthy average citizen. It was also the press. How so? Think about it. If everyone else has their volume forcibly lowered, the one that is still blaring is the only one being heard. The Supreme Court, as we have documented, has neutralized the First Amendment's ability to protect the collective free speech rights of ordinary Americans in our election process. If candidates (particularly nonwealthy challengers) for public office are rendered incapable of getting their message to voters through their own efforts, what is the only other medium through which people will learn about the men and women seeking their vote?

The press is now the third leg of the new power equation of American politics today: incumbents, deep pockets, and the press. These represent today's free speech elite. Prior to *Buckley v. Valeo* and BCRA every citizen and citizen organization had the potential for equal free expression either individually or collectively. Thus factions had the potential to freely counter factions, and special coalitions had the potential to come into being rapidly to voice different emerging points of view. But with a weakened First Amendment this is no longer possible.

Prior to campaign finance reform, editorials and opinion pieces in newspapers, magazines, and the electronic media were often viewed mostly as preaching to their respective choirs. This is to say that the writers and commentators assumed that the majority of those who read the editorial page or saw their programs were familiar with the political persuasion of the newspaper or media outlet. The audience was thus inclined to be sympathetic. As a consequence, there seemed little need for objectivity or fairness.

Yet, with the legalized muzzling of virtually everyone else's speech in the area of politics, the print and electronic media now have acquired significantly more political persuasive power. This means that their editorials and opinions have become substantially more influential. Under campaign finance reform, the press and electronic media have become the last refuge of free expression in politics. There is now a greater need than ever for the press and the electronic media to be more objective and more accurate.

Certainly it is no secret that most of the national press was largely in favor of reform. Yet the truth is that very few editors and commentators had really taken the time or made the effort to fully examine the scope of the issue in its entirety. Instead of doing in-depth research on the subject, too many in the press simply assumed the premise of their argument to be valid. They then applied their considerable rhetorical skill to make the point. Their premise presupposed that their conclusion was true. In classical logic this kind of fallacy is known as "begging the question."

For example, an op-ed piece in one major newspaper argued that the passage of BCRA was crucial to the health of America's political system. In supporting this conclusion, the article asserted that the pork in the 1998 spending bill was payback for campaign contributions. Yet the author offers no concrete evidence to support this allegation. Such unproven claims are a deceptive form of persuasion. While it may be permissible in sales to make inflated claims, they have no place in responsible political journalism. Logical fallacies distort the truth and do nothing to further legitimate dialogue on any political issue. For subjects as serious as elections, free speech, and citizen sovereignty, such specious reasoning should neither be practiced nor tolerated.

It is hoped that the voluminous amount of data presented in this book will demonstrate to everyone in the press, Congress, and the courts that campaign finance reform is *not* a theoretical issue. Instead it is a subject that involves a considerable amount of measurable empirical evidence that can be analyzed and fairly scrutinized by anyone willing to take the time and make the effort to do so. The facts are available to all.

Given that members of the press clearly have a stake in the struggle to reclaim citizen sovereignty, it is important that they now begin to focus their considerable collective talents on scrutinizing the data rather than relying mostly on opinion and demagoguery in attempting to help mold public opinion with regard to money and its impact on politics.

We must leave behind the notion that politics is an evenhanded, tidy, friendly interaction among reasonable people. It is not. Instead, it is a peaceful, but tough and messy, substitute for war. The goal of a political battle is power—sometimes just power itself, but often the power to implement differing agendas based on deeply-held beliefs of what is thought to be the best for our society.

To enable our unique two-party political process to function effectively, the people (the sovereigns) need to be able to freely give and receive, without any government interference, as much input from as many sources as they themselves deem necessary and appropriate, individually or collectively. Each individual is then able to sift through this information, no matter how nasty, jaded, or biased it may appear to be, and obtain what he or she perceives to be the substance. From this seemingly confused hodgepodge, each person is then free to make his or her individual decision as to how to vote. The collective total of everyone's vote expresses the will of the people. This is American democracy in action. And it is an integral part of the checks and balances woven into the Constitution by the Founding Fathers. Only when this often-chaotic process is functioning effectively can the electorate be wise at the polls. Only then can Jefferson and Madison's vision of an informed and involved electorate be fulfilled. Only then can we all be truly free.

15 POLITICAL FUND-RAISING: THE CURRENT REALITY

Congress shall make no law . . . abridging the freedom of speech.

First Amendment to the U.S. Constitution

America's competitive political process is at a crossroads. Its lifeblood, political fund-raising, is under siege. Technological, legislative, and market changes have emerged almost simultaneously to undermine political fund-raising and exponentially increase its complexity and cost. Under the best of circumstances, political fund-raising is a hard sell. These forces of change have made it infinitely more difficult to raise regulated "hard" dollars. But the single most devastating blow to hit political fund-raising is the financial stranglehold imposed by *Buckley v. Valeo*. It has only been made worse by the passage of the Bipartisan Campaign Reform Act (BCRA) and its approval by the Supreme Court.

Without an adequate, continuous supply of money, the political process that was once the best in the world, in fact the best in history, will fall victim to pie-in-the-sky campaign finance reform. This chapter sheds some light on the difficulties involved in political fund-raising as it shifts from a low-volume, high-dollar collection process to a high-volume, lower-dollar collection process. The discussion here is not intended to be a comprehensive analysis but an overview of some of today's realities. While some of the information may seem a bit technical, it is included here to help illuminate the magnitude of the problem.

At the dawn of the twenty-first century, America is still passing through a technological revolution of epic proportions. Thanks to breakthroughs such as the Internet, computerization, telecommunications, robotics, and other evolving technologies, almost every industry, trade, or business activity, including politics, is being affected by this tidal wave of change.

Almost every aspect of industry and business has been diligently attempting to reinvent itself to meet these new challenges. One notable exception is the business of political fund-raising. Compared to the magnitude and variety of change taking place elsewhere, political fund-raising has, for the most part, continued to operate in the same old way. This stagnation has tended to institutionalize modes of fund-raising that are becoming obsolete in the evolving world of contribution limits and high technology.

While campaign finance reform has mandated some of these changes, none of the finance reform laws provide a funding mechanism, other than scarce regulated hard money (raised in compliance with federal law) to pay for the development of systems needed to implement new forms of fund-raising.

To draw an analogy with the commercial world, what campaign finance reform has done to political fund-raising is similar to what would happen if high-priced jewelry were outlawed and Tiffany's immediately had to become a Wal-Mart without access to the financial resources needed to develop the elaborate support systems that enable Wal-Mart to function effectively and efficiently. In other words, political fund-raising is an industry like any other that requires a capital investment in order to go into production.

MARKETS AND MARKETING

Why People Give

Human beings are not angels. They do not give away their hard-earned money for nothing. Whether the cause is political, charitable, or religious, the big question in the back of every donor's mind is always, "What's in it for me if I respond to this request?"

In truth, people trade money to satisfy a basic human need or desire. They trade money to get something. In fund-raising, that something is usually an intangible. Simply stated, fund-raising is the art of motivating people to give money for an intangible or altruistic purpose. This art form deals with feelings, intuition, and motivation. It is an intense form of communication, and it does not happen in neat, logical patterns. Motivating someone to make a contribution only happens when you communicate with that person on a meaningful and emotional level.

Money comes slowly to most people and is usually acquired through hard work and sacrifice. Few people have enough. For most people, making a contribution is a serious matter. Spending or giving money in one direction usually means skimping in another. Consequently, people want value. They want something worth more to them than the same amount spent in another way. That's why political fund-raising is so tough.

Where is the value in giving money to a political organization or to some stranger running for public office? Inducements of some kind are usually essential. The number of people who honestly value political giving more than the alternative uses of their money is very small. Further, the number of identified regular, repeat political donors in America appears to be decreasing, not increasing.

For most Americans, the perceived value of saving someone (especially themselves) from disaster is very high. Thus the most successful political appeals are usually couched in the rhetoric of a crisis or emergency:

> Dear Supporter:
>
> The latest survey shows I am ahead. I should be delighted—but instead I am deeply concerned because lack of cash is slashing my momentum. If I cannot raise $100,000 in the next 20 days, I'll suffer a crushing defeat. That's why I need you to send $25 today.
>
> Sincerely,
> Candidate for Office

While crisis appeals like this can raise a lot of money, most politicians and political organizations don't like even the small amount of negative feedback these appeals also generate. Instead, most politicians and political organizations prefer good news appeals, which seldom have the force to overcome human inertia.

Generally speaking, besides crisis appeals, there are six techniques or thematic approaches for raising money in politics: (1) membership (and the resulting benefits of membership); (2) ego gratification through awards, pictures, and invitations to various kinds of events; (3) perceived or real access to the candidate (incumbent or challenger);(4) appeals based on issues; (5) surveys and petitions; and (6) special premiums.

Obviously, the appropriateness of each of these techniques, particularly access to the candidate, is something the press, the opposition, so-called watchdog groups, and the public are always evaluating and reevaluating. In the final analysis, full and complete disclosure leaves it up to the voters to sift through all available information including fund-raising techniques and contributor lists and then voice their approval or disapproval at the ballot box.

The Current Political Fund-Raising Market

According to the U.S. Census Bureau, the population of the United States in April 2000 was 281,421,906, of which 209,128,094 people were of voting age. In November 2000, a total of 101,452,285 people voted for one of the two major-party presidential candidates (48.5 percent of the eligible voters).

Federal Election Commission (FEC) data show that during the 1999–2000 presidential election cycle, barely 1.5 percent of all Americans gave a campaign contribution to a federal candidate, political party committee, or political action committee. Table 15.1 shows a breakdown of the people nationwide who made a political donation during the 1999–2000 election cycle. The table shows that, as estimated based on a 2000 postelection survey by McLaughlin and Associates, approximately 3.5 million Americans made a political contribution at the federal level during the 1999–2000 election cycle. This figure represents only about 1.3 percent of the total U.S. population and about 1.7 percent of the total voting-age population. Eighty percent of these donors, or roughly 2.7 million people, gave less

Table 15.1 Donors to federal election campaigns, 1999–2000

Giving range	No. of donors	Avg. no. per congressional district	% of population	% of households
≥$1,000	339,526	780	0.1	0.2
$200–$999	439,214	1,010	0.2	0.3
Subtotal ≥$200	778,740	1,790	0.3	0.5
<$200	~2,700,000[a]	6,200	1.0	2.0
All	~3,500,000[a, b]	8,000	1.3	2.5

Source: Numbers of donors giving $200 or more from Federal Election Commission data. Number of donors giving <$200 is an approximation calculated by the author.

[a]Does not include donations made by checking the voluntary presidential campaign donation box on individual federal income tax returns.

[b]In a 2000 postelection survey conducted by McLaughlin and Associates, the base Republican vote for the 2000 presidential election was 38 percent, or roughly 40 million. The base Democratic vote for the 2000 presidential election was 41 percent, or roughly 43 million. This survey also identified known Republican donors to be approximately 5 percent of the Republican base (or about 2 million) and the known Democratic donors to be approximately 3 percent of the Democrat base (or about 1.5 million), for a combined Republican/Democrat donor base of approximately 3.5 million.

than two hundred dollars. These smaller contributions are the most time-consuming and expensive to raise.

There is roughly 1 donor (Republican, Democrat, or independent) of $200 or more for every 350 people (0.3 percent), or 1 in every 200 households (0.5 percent) in the average congressional district. This means that under the mandated contribution restrictions, trying to raise significant amounts of money in any given congressional district for a political party or candidate is like trying to find a finite number of needles in the proverbial haystack. And for challengers without wealth, the task of raising enough money from small donors to defeat an incumbent ranges between virtually to completely impossible.

The estimate of 3.5 million total donors represents a reasonable approximation of the entire known universe of political donors in America. These people supply *all* of the individual donor money for *all* of the committees and candidates—for all national, state, and local party committees and all federal-reporting political action committees for all presidential, congressional, and state and local campaigns, for Republicans, Democrats, and Independents across the country. It is a frightfully small supply of proven hard-money donors for a relatively large pool of fund-raisers with an inexhaustible demand. Thus it is not surprising that intraparty competition for dollars is often as competitive and as intense as the interparty competition for votes.

The Changing Political Fund-Raising Market

At the time of *Buckley v. Valeo* in 1976, the dominant audience for mass marketing in America was the "patriot generation," consisting of people born before 1925. The year 1925 is important because it is the last year an individual could have been born and suffered through the Depression and been old enough to fight in World War II, both of which were life-altering experiences.

Think what America was like prior to 1925. No television, no Internet, few phones, some cars, and lots of small towns. Children raised during this era were generally taught to believe that their role as citizens was to make society better. They joined groups like the Boy Scouts and Girl Scouts; they respected authority, leadership, and civic-mindedness. Growing up in a national small-town culture gave them a sense of civic duty and patriotism. As they aged, they volunteered and donated money because it was consistent with their self-image.

Over 53 million Americans born prior to 1925 were alive in 1976.[1] As children, this generation looked at such things as Sears and Roebuck and Montgomery Ward catalogs for entertainment as well as for shopping. Their personal communication was by letters, and their mass communication was through newspapers, magazines, billboards, and catalogs. They were accustomed to doing things through the mail. When the political contribution limits first went into effect in 1976, this generation was largely an untapped source of political giving. Direct-mail appeals to the patriot generation audience became an important source of new money and helped offset some of the sting imposed by the new financial restrictions. Subsequent to *Buckley v. Valeo,* this patriot generation audience became the financial backbone for most political organizations. Prior to *Buckley v. Valeo,* most financial support for political campaigns came from a smaller number of larger contributions. Obtaining larger contributions from fewer donors was and still is the least expensive way to quickly raise substantial sums of money.

Now, at the start of a new century, most of the patriot generation has disappeared and, along with them, a substantial source of reliable revenue for political organizations. Most of the political financial support today comes from the generation born between 1926 and 1945. Psychologically, this transition generation shares traits with both the patriot generation and the later baby boomer generation (born between 1946 and 1964).

The transition generation's parents drilled the lessons of the Great Depression into the heads of their children. Thus people born between 1926 and 1945 tend to be organization-loyal and value-oriented. They resemble their parents in that they tend to give generously to charity. The problem with this transition generation for fund-raisers is its size; it represents only about 15 percent of the population.[2] So as a source of political funding, its potential is limited.

The most important fund-raising market today is the huge baby boomer generation (more than 70 million adults), whose propensity for giving to political organizations and candidates is still largely unknown. Equally troubling is the fact that marketing techniques and tools to entice boomers to make political contributions are also largely undeveloped. Boomers were told that life is a voyage of self-discovery and that they could do anything they wanted. The data suggest that they are inherently optimistic and imbued with a sense of entitlement to the good life, which tends to make them self-centered.[3] They are the only generation that withdrew from a war (Vietnam) and brought down a president (Johnson). They grew up watching lots of television and using the telephone extensively. They tend to buy first and pay later, using credit cards and monthly payment plans. They've grown up with TV advertising and are comfortable with transacting business over the telephone. In short, the psychological profile of the baby boomer generation is far different from that of their patriot generation elders.

The Changing Techniques of Marketing

As a result of this shift in profiles from the patriot generation to the baby boomer generation, the old mass-marketing political fund-raising methodologies, including the use of mass media, mass mailing, and even mass telemarketing, are slowly giving way to a radically new marketing paradigm specifically targeted at boomers and the younger emerging markets. These new marketing techniques are best explained simply as "one-to-one" marketing. Instead of raising money through mass mailings to a single homogeneous group like the patriot generation, we are heading toward a time when to be successful at fund-raising, political organizations and candidates will have to be able to generate more customized, individualized appeals. Books like *The One to One Future* and *Enterprise One to One* by Don Peppers and Martha Rogers, *The Next Economy* by Elliott Ettenberg, and *Defining Markets, Defining Moments* by Geoffrey E. Meredith and Charles D. Schewe all discuss various aspects of this emerging reality. An example of the marketing change now taking place in politics is the decline in money being raised by direct mail and the increase in money being raised from the transition generation and the leading edge of the baby boomer generation through telemarketing.

To meet these new marketing demands and this emerging marketing paradigm, political organizations and candidates will have to be able to access communication systems that enable them to interact with people on the issues that are important to each individual through the medium preferred by each individual. I have coined the phrase *tri-marketing* to describe this new, evolving marketing concept.

Tri-Marketing

Tri-marketing involves the process of integrating and coordinating the three most widely used forms of mass personalized communications in such a way that each communication is specifically tailored to the individual recipient. The three mass-marketing media of tri-marketing are direct mail, telemarketing (both inbound and outbound), and the Internet (including e-mail and Web sites). The successful implementation of tri-marketing would help candidates and political organizations forge closer ties with donors and supporters, recruit volunteers, dispense up-to-the-minute information, promote political activism, and, of course, raise money.

Tri-marketing, or something similar, or perhaps even more advanced, is the wave of the future. However, campaign finance laws block access to the financial resources and cooperative business relationships necessary for candidates and political committees to effectively maximize the development of such highly sophisticated marketing systems. As a consequence, every political entity's ability to compete in the evolving new fund-raising world is going to be hampered by restrictive laws and regulations.

The Howard Dean Campaign

During the 2004 Democratic presidential primary, Howard Dean's fund-raising effort successfully utilized a rudimentary form of tri-marketing. Dean's campaign raised a significant amount of money by integrating the use of the Internet, direct mail, and telephones to accomplish both political and fund-raising objectives. Traditionally, political campaigns have tended to keep their fund-raising and political communications separate. So Dean's systematic integration of political and fund-raising messages was a fresh, innovative approach to raising money in politics.

Table 15.2 shows the approximate number of people nationwide who made a contribution to Dean's campaign, along with the average number of donors per congressional district and the percentage of the population and of households this number represents, broken down by giving range. These data give a sense of the magnitude of the challenge Dean's fund-raising team faced and overcame.

In total, Howard Dean's campaign recruited some 350,000 donors and raised approximately $53 million dollars. To accomplish this feat, the campaign had to figure out how to recruit cost effectively an average of some 807 donors per congressional district, with each donor giving an average of about $150.

Cost-effectively recruiting 807 donors out of an average of 600,000 people in a congressional district is a daunting task and an impressive accomplishment, especially when you consider that 807 people is only thirteen one-hundredths of one percent (0.13 percent) of the average number of people living in any given district.

Table 15.2 Donors to Dean presidential campaign, 2003–2004

Giving range	No. of donors	Avg. no. per congressional district	Avg. per 100,000 population	Avg. per 100,000 households
≥$1,000	9,800	23	4	7
$200–$999	60,200	140	23	47
Subtotal ≥$200	70,000	163	27	54
< $200	280,000	644	107	184
All	350,000[a]	807	135	230

Source: Estimates based on Federal Election Commission data and information provided by Dean campaign staff.
[a]Verbally confirmed by the Dean campaign.

But there was a catch to Dean's fund-raising success. For the Dean campaign to raise such a large sum of money in limited amounts in a relatively short period of time, the candidate had to take very strong positions on some highly controversial issues. Thus while the touting of highly charged emotional issues helped Dean raise lots of money, it also made him vulnerable to charges of demagoguery or extremism that had the potential to hurt his campaign politically. One of the fund-raising lessons to be learned from the Dean campaign is that if a candidate is not an incumbent or does not have a significant amount of personal wealth, then he or she really has no choice under campaign finance reform but to aggressively pursue controversial issues to raise any significant amount of money.

MODES OF FUND-RAISING

The four most commonly used ways to ask an individual for money are by letter (direct mail), (2) by telephone, (3) face-to-face (through a finance committee), and (4) e-mail. As the volume of people contacted through one or more of these modes of fund-raising increases, the nature of the fund-raising effort changes. It should also be noted that events (dinners, receptions, cocktail parties, etc.), which are an integral part of political fund-raising, are technically a benefit or reward for giving, not a mode of fund-raising per se.

Volume Changes Form

As the size of something increases, its form tends to change. For example, the various functions that occur within a typical congressional campaign often look substantially the same as corresponding functions in a presidential campaign. But they are not necessarily the same. At some point, the sheer numbers involved in a particular function will force a change in its form.

A simple example of this dynamic is the function of processing contributions. Every campaign has to process checks. Yet a clerk processing two thousand checks over the course of a congressional campaign has a far different kind of system than the check-processing system for a presidential campaign that receives several hundred thousand checks over the same time period. This principle of volume changing form affects every aspect of fund-raising, particularly as political fund-raising scrambles to offset the loss of large contributions.

It stands to reason that as the average contribution declines, the number of contributions needed to generate the same funds increases, as does the cost of generating the necessary number of contributions. To make up for lost revenue resulting from the imposition of contribution limits, the volume of smaller contributions must increase as the average contribution amount declines. This dynamic results in unavoidably higher fund-raising costs. In fact, there is an inverse relationship between fund-raising costs and average contribution. The higher the average contribution, the lower fund-raising costs will be as a percentage of gross receipts. The reverse is also true. The lower the average contribution, the higher the fund-raising cost will be. Table 15.3 shows the cost of raising $1 million from various numbers of donors.

Table 15.3. Cost of raising $1 million from various numbers of donors

	NUMBER OF DONORS			
	1	1,000	10,000	100,000
Average gift required for $1 million total	$1,000,000	$1,000	$100	$10
Cost per donation[a]	$5	$5	$5	$5
Total donation cost	$5	$5,000	$50,000	$500,000
Donation cost percentage	0.0005%	0.5%	5%	50%
Acquisition cost per donor[a]	$10	$10	$10	$10
Total donor acquisition cost	$10	$10,000	$100,000	$1,000,000
Combined total cost	$15	$15,000	$150,000	$1,500,000
Cost percentage	0.0015%	1.5%	15%	150%

[a]Estimate for illustration purposes only.

Each of the examples in Table 15.3 has its own special fund-raising challenge. Attempting to get $1 million from one person is a radically different fund-raising challenge than attempting to get $10 each from 100,000 people. The human effort, the cost, the mode of fund-raising used, the support systems needed, and the time involved are all different for each example shown. The interactive relationships between cost, volume, and the average contribution also differs for each mode of fund-raising.

Donor Acquisition

The cost dynamic of fund-raising is further complicated by the fact that every fund-raising organization must also spend money acquiring new donors.

Given that the active donor audience for most political organizations is relatively fixed, there are only two ways a fund-raising operation can grow. One is by increasing the average contribution. The other is by prospecting for more donors. Because the mandated contribution limits imposed by campaign finance reform severely limit every political organization's ability to increase its average contribution amount, the only alternative for generating additional revenue is to acquire more donors.

This process of acquiring new donors is commonly referred to as "prospecting." The initial goal of prospecting is merely to break even, which means the entire cost of acquiring new donors is recouped by their first contribution. However, breaking even at prospecting is a difficult objective to achieve. In fact, it is often impossible. In such situations, donor growth must be partially funded out of general operating funds. Unfortunately, few people understand the fact that money must be spent to acquire new donors, which invariably leads to a misconception that fund-raising expenditures are unnecessarily high.

In addition to the direct cost of soliciting each contribution, then, Table 15.3 also shows a total cost assuming an acquisition cost of ten dollars per donor. Thus the total cost to raise $1 million from one donor is fifteen dollars, a very good return on investment. But when the same cost factor of five dollars per gift and ten dollars for donor acquisition is applied to 100,000 donors, the total fund-raising cost is $1.5 million, half again as much as the assumed gross receipts in this example. Clearly, a candidate would have great difficulty relying on ten-dollar donations to finance a campaign.

The reason for the huge variance between these examples is the unavoidable functional relationship between donor volume and average contribution and cost. As volume and the average contribution amount change, so do the cost and the form of the fund-raising challenge. As these examples clearly demonstrate, the aggregate fund-raising cost as a percentage of gross receipts increases as volume increases and the average contribution drops. Indeed, volume does change form.

Mathematical Realities

By imposing contribution limits on candidates and political organizations, campaign finance reform has mandated a lower average contribution amount, which necessitates a need to significantly increase volume in order to make up the lost revenue. Thus the imposed financial restrictions and limits have increased every political institution's fund-raising cost.

It might be argued that the increase in the allowable hard-money contribution amounts included in BCRA has mitigated the harsh reality of this mathematical dynamic at least in part. However, in terms of real purchasing power, the increased contribution limits are deceptive. Take for example the individual giving limit to candidates. BCRA increased it from $1,000 to $2,000, a 100 percent increase. Yet this increase is not as significant as it seems. According to the Bureau of Labor Statistics' Inflation Calculator (at www.bls.gov/cpi/home.htm), the inflation factor for 2004 relative to 1976 dollars was 332 percent. By 2004 the old individual contribution limit of $1,000 was worth only $301 in 1976 dollars, and the new individual contribution limit of $2,000 was really only worth $602 in 1976 dollars. Thus the new contribution limits incorporated in BCRA are not really increases because they do not make up for the loss in purchasing power due to inflation.

Direct Mail

In politics, direct mail is the most common way, as of this writing, to raise money from a large audience. In its simplest form, mass marketing by direct mail involves sending out a large volume of letters to a targeted audience. To send one mailing, at a cost of fifty cents per letter, to a target audience of every household in an average congressional district (typically about 350,000 households), the resulting cost would be approximately $175,000 (350,000 × $0.50). Table 15.4 shows the response rates and

Table 15.4 Breakeven analysis for districtwide household mailing costing $175,000

Average gift	Response rate	No. of donors per 350,000
$25	2%	7,000
$50	1%	3,500
$100	0.5%	1,750

numbers of donors that would be required for such a mailing to break even at various average contribution levels.

The numbers in this table look deceptively simple, perhaps even achievable. But considering that prospecting to premium rental lists of known donors who have contributed to other political causes usually generates a response of only around 1 to 2 percent, it becomes apparent that breaking even on a mailing to a compiled list of non-donors in a congressional district would be virtually impossible without the aid of some highly sophisticated screening process. And even then it is very difficult. A response of even 0.2 percent with an average contribution of $25 from an unscreened list would be a remarkable accomplishment. Yet such a response would generate less than $20,000 in total revenue for an entire congressional district. At the 2002 bulk mailing rate of twenty cents per letter, this amount would not even cover postage ($70,000 to reach 350,000 households).

Thus direct mail is a high-volume, high-cost, and low-yield source of revenue that requires time and qualified professional management to be effective, and as campaign finance reform has intensified its use, over-solicitation is reducing its effectiveness.

Telemarketing

The telephone is something everyone in America is familiar with. Just pick up the receiver and call a friend. It's that simple. Or is it? From the point of view of fund-raising, the process gets complicated very quickly.

Telemarketing is a two-way form of communication. Because the telephone is highly personal, it is an effective way to motivate people to give money. But as volume increases, state-of-the-art technology becomes necessary. Good management and sophisticated technology are the only ways to maximize the productivity and cost-effectiveness of telemarketing.

As a general rule, it takes about three dials to get one answered phone call (i.e., a connected call) and two answered phone calls to make one completed call (i.e., to talk with the person you are trying to contact). This means it takes an average of six dials to complete one call. At that rate, to complete a call to every household in an average congressional district (i.e., approximately 350,000 households) it would take about 2.1 million calls. As the number of calls increases, things like wrong phone numbers, busy signals, unanswered calls, and answering machines all become very important because they consume time, money, and manpower. Moreover, a phone call only secures a commitment. Converting a phone commitment to cash involves an entirely separate process.

Given the very few mass-marketing options available, campaign finance reform has necessitated a significant increase in the use of telemarketing for political fund-raising. However, the increased use of cell phones (whose numbers are not yet listed in phone directories) and electronic screening devises and the increase in government regulation are adding to the complexity and cost of telemarketing.

Finance Committees

A finance committee is made up of volunteers who solicit contributions from their friends, business associates, and relatives in a one-on-one, person-to-person fund-raising effort. The finance committee concept is the traditional backbone of major-donor fund-raising in politics. The range of prospects for the average member of a finance committee is usually between fifteen and forty people. These prospects are the people a finance committee member usually sees or speaks to by phone at least once or twice a month. If the finance committee is diligent and persuasive, its success rate can range between 25 and 50 percent. Occasionally, a superstar emerges who exceeds this range, but such people are hard to find.

The imposition of contribution limits has introduced a new twist to the finance committee concept. It is called "bundling." There are two forms of bundling. One is legal, and the other is questionable at best and illegal at worst. In the first form, a finance committee is created to raise money for several candidates instead of only one, and the donors, including PACs, are asked to write checks to a number of different candidates. This kind of bundling operation usually involves appeals to controversial, emotional issues.

In the more questionable form of bundling, a person in a position of authority, usually an executive, coerces people under his or her control to make contributions they might not otherwise make. In rare cases, such forced contributions are illegally reimbursed. In any event, the practice of compelling people to make contributions against their will is a sad reminder of the lengths people will go to circumvent the contribution limits in attempting to exercise their disappearing rights of free speech.

The few people interested in political fund-raising are generally much more willing to write a check than they are to ask a friend, associate, or relatives for money. Therefore recruiting finance committee members is seldom easy. Raising money through finance committees usually has limited potential in politics, especially for challenger candidates, given the severe contribution restrictions imposed by campaign finance reform. They can be effective, however, for incumbent candidates and in those few special situations where a campaign, candidate, or issue receives a lot of free publicity or when a finance committee has truly exceptional leadership.

The Internet

Because the Internet is evolving so rapidly, it is difficult to evaluate its ultimate impact on political fund-raising. At the present time, e-mail is the single-most powerful tool on the Internet. It is a cheap, efficient way to deliver content. It's also a great way for people of similar interests to communicate. And while there have been a number of notable Internet fund-raising successes, most of the big money raised so far has been the direct result of candidates and/or causes benefitting from a huge amount of free and/or paid publicity. Without the media frenzy, the Internet has not as yet demonstrated it can generate a large, *continuous* flow of ongoing, reliable income. How its use will evolve is still unclear, but there is absolutely no doubt that the Internet has a bright future in political fund-raising.

Yet fund-raising is not just about soliciting contributions. It is also about developing and keeping relationships with donors, which is one of the keys to long-term, cost-effective fund-raising success. The Internet's ability to help forge a relationship with donors is quickly evolving. One exciting fund-raising possibility for the Internet involves the development of a sophisticated communications system that can deliver customized messages to each donor or supporter and send and answer messages via the individual's preferred communication channel (mail, telephone, or email). Unfortunately, the problem of spam, the general bombardment of unwanted messages, the ease of blocking unsolicited e-mail, and the ever-evolving efforts to control spam are making the process of reaching donors and supporters more difficult.

As the Internet continues to mature and the Internet population becomes more mainstream in profile, Web sites and e-mail communications will have to become more personalized to remain potent, widely used fund-raising tools. Unfortunately, keeping pace with ever-changing Internet technology is going to cost money, and lots of it. Thanks to *Buckley v. Valeo* and BCRA, as the Internet continues to evolve and gain in complexity and sophistication, it is going to be a real struggle for political organizations and candidates to find the money to invest in this cutting-edge technology.

Other Modes of Fund-Raising

Recurring Payments

The least expensive way to collect a large number of small contributions from individuals is through automatic, recurring payments by electronic funds transfer, credit and debit cards, and payroll deductions. Unfortunately, for a variety of reasons, these modes of automatic collection are not a practical alternative for most political organizations or candidates. The most notable exception to this general rule is the money raised by corporate PACs and labor organizations through payroll deduction, which is one reason corporate and union fund-raising operations are so powerful and profitable. If they can be established and maintained, these automated modes of collection are efficient, inexpensive ways to raise significant amounts of money on a continuing basis.

Political Action Committees

PACs are anomalies created by Congress to funnel money into politics. Any entity such as a corporation, union, or nonprofit organization can create a PAC. In fact any individual or group of individuals can start a PAC. However, once in existence every PAC must register with the FEC and comply with all the relevant rules and limits mandated by federal election law.

When candidates and party committees attempt to raise money from PACs, the rules of fund-raising persuasion rarely apply. The reason for this is that virtually everything about a PAC is pragmatic. There is almost no human emotion involved the process by which a PAC decides how and where to contribute its money. This is why PACs are not really a mode of fund-raising per se. As mentioned earlier, the art of fund-raising involves communicating with people on a meaningful and emotional level. Success in getting money from PACs involves virtually none of this. That's why

Table 15.5 Distribution of PAC contributions to incumbents, challengers, and open-seat candidates

	2002	2000	1998	1996	1994	1992
Incumbents	76%	75%	78%	67%	72%	72%
Challengers	10%	11%	10%	15%	10%	12%
Open-seat candidates	14%	14%	12%	18%	18%	16%

Source: Federal Election Commission news release, March 27, 2003.

raising money from PACs is more like a collection process than a fund-raising effort.

A March 2003 news release from the FEC shows that 4,594 PACs distributed on average in excess of $100,000 each during the course of 2001–2002 election cycle.[4] Table 15.5 shows the percentage of all PAC contributions distributed to incumbents, challengers, and candidates for open seats in six election cycles (1992–2002).

It is obvious from these FEC numbers that few challengers can count on financial support from the PAC community when they run against incumbents. Thus, while PACs are readily available and inexpensive to communicate with (at fifty cents per letter, a mailing to the entire PAC community costs less than $2,500), PACs are not a reliable source of funding for anyone except incumbents, some few open seats, an occasional challenger, and some party committees in limited amounts.

Since PACs set up their own predetermined criteria for giving, neither the strength of a candidate's appeal nor a candidate's need for money carries any significant weight with PACs. While it might be helpful to have the right people asking a PAC for support, in the final analysis, a PAC's unique criteria must be met to get money. If that criterion is not met, a candidate will seldom if ever get money from a PAC.

When the various fund-raising challenges outlined in this chapter are considered along with the other factors discussed in this book, such as the repressive contribution restrictions, limitations on the placement of campaign ads by both citizens and citizen groups, and the stiff penalties that can be imposed for violations, it should be obvious why incumbents and wealthy candidates will dominate the new political landscape created by campaign finance reform and why the competitive nature of elections in America is disappearing. America's proud heritage of free speech and open elections has been unknowingly supplanted by unfree speech and closed elections, all in the name of reform. If campaign finance reform remains to law of the land, it may not be long before elections in America are little more than incumbent coronations and our Supreme Court–mandated plebeian class has little more to do with government than to begrudgingly obey its laws.

16 THE TWENTY-EIGHTH AMENDMENT

Fourscore and seven years ago our fathers brought forth on this continent a new nation, conceived in liberty and dedicated to the proposition that all men are created equal. . . . [W]e here highly resolve that these dead shall not have died in vain, that this nation under God shall have a new birth of freedom, and that government of the people, by the people, for the people shall not perish from the earth.

Abraham Lincoln, Gettysburg Address

In his Gettysburg Address, Abraham Lincoln equated what was happening in the Civil War with the founding of the nation. In this short, powerful speech, Lincoln was able to change the meaning of the Civil War. After Gettysburg, the war was no longer simply about preserving the Union. Henceforth the war would be about "a new birth of freedom." Lincoln's commitment to and faith in the ideals embodied in the Declaration of Independence was so strong that even with the nation's survival still in doubt, he boldly elevated that terrible struggle to a higher moral plane.

During the Civil War, America was going through a catharsis, attempting to hold two different views of what the Declaration of Independence stood for. Southerners cited their freedom to secede as the colonists had done when the regime of King George became too oppressive. Lincoln spoke of a more profound freedom—an end to slavery, which the Constitution had legitimized. Both sides paid a heavy price trying to cling to their own views of freedom.

By reaffirming the doctrine of equality, Lincoln was moving the country away from a limited interpretation of constitutional principles toward a more inclusive one. In effect, he was extending citizen sovereignty to those who were enslaved. He had already issued the Emancipation Proclamation, freeing the slaves in the Confederate states. The Gettysburg Address was an implicit promise to the enslaved people in the five slaveholding Union states.

To make his expanded vision of citizen sovereignty a reality, Lincoln had to initiate and secure the ratification of the Thirteenth Amendment, ending slavery. Yet as compelling as the circumstances were to put an end to slavery at that moment in our history, it still took all the power of the presidency and the euphoria following Lincoln's reelection in 1864 to get the Thirteenth Amendment through Congress. In fact, the amendment passed the House of Representative by just three votes more than the required two-thirds majority.

Contrast what Abraham Lincoln did in just one speech at Gettysburg with what the Supreme Court did in just one opinion in the aftermath of Watergate. In 1972, America was once again going through a purification process—nothing as catastrophic or destructive as a civil war, but still a painful, wrenching experience for the entire nation. This time the crisis was about abuse of power—the very thing the Framers most feared. Thankfully, the system of checks and balances the Founding Fathers had woven into the Constitution resolved the Watergate conflict. In a testament to the Framer's foresight and genius, the system worked.

However, after the Watergate hearings had concluded, there was still a lingering sense of doubt and vulnerability throughout the country. This uneasiness aroused the instinct of self-preservation within the halls of Congress. How would Americans vent their pent-up frustration? One obvious possibility was that they might take it out on their respective representatives in Congress.

To guard against any threat to their own reelection, Congress disregarded Madison's warning in Federalist 10 (discussed in Chapter 5) about not risking the destruction of everyone's freedom by restricting certain factions' access to the entire political process, and passed the Federal Election Campaign Act. Among other things, this legislation imposed restrictions on campaign contributions and expenditures, even though an earlier Supreme Court, in its 1921 *Newberry v. United States* opinion, had already ruled limits on expenditures unconstitutional.

Knowing the consequences, it is hard to look back today and see this repressive piece of legislation as anything other than a defensive, self-serving cynical act. Even as the legislation was being drafted, most on Capitol Hill knew some of its major provisions were unconstitutional. As soon as this bill became law, several parties challenged its constitutionality.

The stage was now set for the Supreme Court's *Buckley v. Valeo* decision. Like Lincoln's Gettysburg Address, the consequences of *Buckley v. Valeo* were monumental, but in a vastly different way. Speaking for just three minutes and using only 272 words, Abraham Lincoln expanded the founding principles of equality and freedom. The Supreme Court, by contrast, took 28,272 words to create a new form of inequality.

Without a single shot being fired, the Supreme Court, like Lincoln, created a new nation. But the High Court's new nation was one of regression, not progress. The Court's revisionist view of citizen sovereignty was exclusionary and limiting. Like the system of ancient Rome, *Buckley v. Valeo* had the unintended consequence of rigging elections in favor of the rich. No longer were all American citizens equal under the law.

Future historians are likely to look back on January 30, 1976—the day the Supreme Court announced its *Buckley v. Valeo* decision—as one of the most regrettable moments in American history. It was the moment when our competitive two-party electoral process was ordered by the Supreme Court to surrender its cherished freedom. America elections were forced to enter an uncharted political no-man's-land controlled by the federal government.

Twenty-six years later, Congress became very alarmed about the amount and intensity of criticism directed at its members. Emotionally charged, highly effective commercials in the form of "issue ads" sponsored by individuals, advocacy groups, and party committees had become the new fad. Although these ads did not specifically urge viewers to vote for or against any member of Congress, they were most certainly designed to influence elections. Such ads represented the kind of political discourse that was once extolled in civics classes as free speech.

However, given the latest triumph of political correctness over the Constitution in Congress, this kind of speech was now seen as an opportunity for corruption or the perception of corruption, particularly if large donations were underwriting the cost of such statements. Adding fuel to the fire, the national media rallied support for the whole idea of "the perception of corruption" with a steady, continuous barrage of sensationalized journalism. Of the nation's top ten newspapers as of September 30, 2003—*USA Today* (circulation 2,154,539), the *Wall Street Journal* (2,091,062), the *New York Times* (1,118,565), the *Los Angeles Times* (914,584), the *Washington Post* (732,872), the *New York Daily News* (729,124), the *Chicago Tribune* (680,879), the *New York Post* (652,426), *Newsday* (580,069), and the *Houston Chronicle* (553,048)[1]—eight supported campaign finance reform.

The *Houston Chronicle* is middle-of-the-road, and the *Wall Street Journal* was anti-reform.

The *Wall Street Journal*'s editorial stance has consistently been wary of the reform craze. With editorial titles such as "Doubting Thomas," "A Self-Serving Senate," and "Campaign Fairy Tale,"[2] the *Journal* is direct and consistent in its position as an advocate of the First Amendment and a foe of campaign finance reform.

According to Jonathan Chait, a senior editor at the *New Republic*, "Media coverage of campaign finance shamelessly touts reform." He notes, "Almost every finance story features quotes from campaign finance reform advocates . . . without any counterbalancing quotes from reform foes."[3]

Rep. Steve Largent (R-OK) gave an another explanation for the mainstream media's support of the Bipartisan Campaign Reform Act (BCRA):

> In a McCain-Feingold [BCRA] world, media elites would be allowed to freely mention a federal candidate by name in the weeks leading up to an election, but other citizens would not be allowed to do so. Media elites would of course be allowed to freely advocate timely issues in the media in the weeks leading up to an election, but other citizens would not be allowed to do so. And media elites would be allowed to consult with congressmen without restriction in the weeks leading up to an election, but other citizens would not be allowed to do so. Is it any surprise that media elites support the McCain-Feingold bill? They are totally exempt and no one else is.[4]

Because the media are not subject to the same campaign finance regulations as nonmedia corporations, "newspapers, magazines, TV and radio corporations can spend unlimited sums to promote the election of favored candidates," says Bradley Smith in *Unfree Speech*.[5] According to Bruce Buchanan, author of *Presidential Campaign Quality*, the media's "unmatched access to mass public attention" and "near monopoly of the airwaves and print space" make the media very influential in shaping the news agenda and public opinion.[6] As ABC News reported, "Critics of the [campaign finance reform] legislation denounce it as an unacceptable intrusion on the First Amendment, but most editorialists have been unmoved by those concerns. Newspapers are usually staunch defenders of free speech rights. But in this debate, most newspapers have turned aside the objections of free speech advocates like the ACLU and sided instead with those who favor greater government regulation of political fund-raising and advertising."[7]

Editorials in the *Washington Post* consistently showed the newspaper supported campaign finance reform.[8] At least twenty-two *New York Times* editorials from January to April 2001 referred to campaign finance reform. While the *Times* did, according to ABC News, "raise constitutional questions about applying the pre-election issue-ad restriction to interest groups," the newspaper's editorials "heartily endorsed McCain-Feingold [BCRA]."[9] On March 27, 2001, the *Times* editorial department stated: "This page, which has a record of vigilance on the First Amendment, is convinced that nothing in the core McCain-Feingold bill, including its curbs on fund-raising for so-called issue ads by independent groups, would violate the Constitution."[10]

Once all the negative media hype over campaign finance reform had convinced enough members of Congress that big contributions to virtually any political entity were corruptive, or at least possibly corruptive, a majority in Congress again put on their "white hats" and brazenly passed BCRA in 2002. This act helped insulate incumbents from criticism, particularly from issue ads sponsored by national parties and paid for with soft money. This further reduced the possibility of their being defeated because nonwealthy challenger candidates were cut off from a cost-effective way of communicating with voters.

The following year, on December 10, 2003, the Supreme Court once again pointedly ignored the Constitution (as well as the ideals it embodies) and declared all the major provisions of BCRA constitutional. Utilizing legal gymnastics for expedience, the High Court rationalized that money is inherently corrupting and that by limiting the amount of money and the timing of speech, somehow the entire political process would become more virtuous. The Court's declaring BCRA constitutional gave redundant proof of the breakdown in our unique constitutional form of government. It was a symbol as well as a symptom of our loss of citizen sovereignty.

Can nothing be done to restore to the citizens the sovereignty they have lost, or surrendered, to federal authority? This question is particularly poignant when one realizes that few Americans today understand that they have lost anything. Part of the problem may be our loss of memory as a people. Or perhaps it's that academia has focused too much on historical tends and the achievements of society as a whole and too little on the acts of great men like the Founding Fathers. Or it could be that too many of us simply learned our history in school badly or not at all.

Whatever the reason, our collective lack of a fundamental understanding of history is sad because the study of history, especially American history, teaches us the values, rights, and responsibilities of our citizenship. A strong case can also be made that the reason we are allowing our precious citizen sovereignty to slip away is that neither journalists nor the public have a clear understanding of how campaign finance reform has actually affected elections.

This latter reason is primarily why I wrote this book. I think the editorial staff of the *New York Times* and other proreform news outlets sincerely believe that campaign finance reform is a good idea and that it will work. The tragedy is that they have arrived at this conclusion without the benefit of all the relevant facts. Most journalists and the vast majority of the general public simply aren't aware of the data or the negative consequences of campaign finance reform presented in this book.

Politicians benefit from this lack of general awareness: few other undertakings allow them to ensure their job security while taking on the appearance of acting in the voters' interest. Consequently, Congress is unlikely to undo what it has done so efficiently to increase control over its own destiny. Had members of Congress laid out an agenda with the specific goal of ensuring their own reelection, they could not have fashioned a better ruse. Each new "reform" has further secured Capitol Hill against the siege of candidates who, in their idealism and ignorance, still believe they have the right to seriously challenge and in some cases even unseat an incumbent.

With all the legislation, precedents, and court decisions in place, even a Supreme Court packed with strict constructionists would probably be reluctant to strike down the formidable body of legal rationalization that now controls our election process. At the moment, the High Court's word seems to be final, at least on constitutional matters.

But the truth is that something *can* be done to correct what is now a serious flaw in the electoral process. As already noted, when earlier political leaders wanted to make changes in the way federal elections were conducted, they felt obliged to amend the Constitution. Like Lincoln, other great American leaders have endeavored to expand and enhance citizen sovereignty by amending the Constitution.

In this manner, former slaves were guaranteed the right to vote (1870), as were women (1920) and eighteen-year-olds (1971). Once chosen by state legislatures, senators are now elected by popular vote (1913), again, the result of an amendment. The poll tax was abolished in the same manner (1964), and citizens of the District of Colombia were given the right to vote in presidential elections (1961).

Given the barnacle-like increase of laws restricting the way citizens conduct their elections, only a constitutional amendment can remove Congress and the Court's invasion of our democratic process and return the power to the people.

Here is that amendment.

Proposed Twenty-eighth Amendment

In terms of elections, the People's and the Press's right to know and voice opinion is absolute! And while it remains the government's responsibility to proscribe the time, place, and manner of holding elections that are open, fair and free from corruption, Congress shall make no law restricting the right of citizens to form political parties and other organizations for the purpose of electing candidates to federal office, to finance federal election campaigns, or to use collected funds for the exercise of free political speech in federal campaigns, though Congress may enact laws that require full financial disclosure by political campaign organizations.

Such an amendment would effectively prevent Congress and the federal judiciary from restricting citizens' right to free speech, their right to assemble peaceably, or their ability to finance campaigns for public office. The process would be returned to where it was at the beginning of the republic, when James Madison and others were willing to risk the domination of factions or special interests in order to maintain a newly won citizen sovereignty.

What would be the effect of such an amendment on the current electoral process?

Would huge corporations and labor unions pour money into federal election campaigns in order to influence the outcome? Not necessarily. Since 1907, federal law has prohibited corporate contributions in federal elections. In 1947 Congress passed a similar ban on contributions by unions. The principle behind these laws has nothing to do with citizen sovereignty. Corporations and unions are granted special legal privileges by government so that they can serve the greater good of our economy. The wealth they amass from these privileges should not be used to give them an unfair advantage in the political arena. In addition, neither corporations nor unions have ever been granted the privilege to vote as individual citizens. Thus the government has the right to regulate them in ways not appropriate for individuals.

Will the superrich have as much political influence as they do now? In some respects they will. They are citizens under the Constitution and as such enjoy the same protection due every citizen. Under the proposed amendment they would be allowed to share and commingle their wealth with ordinary citizens, strengthening both our two-party political process and the voice of candidates without wealth. Under the current rules, the wealthy can spend as much as they choose on issue ads and on themselves as candidates; they simply have to spend it under their own auspices or through an independent 527 entity rather than through a political party or campaign organization. If the proposed amendment were ratified, much of this money would flow, fully disclosed, through political party and candidate committees. Given full disclosure, voters would be able to judge for themselves the merit of larger contributions.

Will the system be even more susceptible to greater corruption? In the first place, no one has proved that political contributions were corrupting under the old rules. There is certainly a general perception of corruption among elected officials, but this perception is due in greater part to relentless hype and sensationalism than to consideration of facts. It has always been against the law to trade legislative favors for contributions. The trading of legislative favor for contributions should be policed through various improved forms of full disclosure and punished to the fullest extent of the law when it occurs.

Considering that, under the current restrictions, special interests and wealthy individuals can still support candidates and issues either through independent expenditures or through 527 groups, how could their participation be any more corrupting under the proposed amendment? One of the things people generally fail to realize is that none of the congressional or court-ordered contribution restrictions stop corporations, unions, or the wealthy elite from spending all the money they care to on politics.

All the campaign finance reform laws have done is restrict the flow of money to political party committees and candidates without wealth. Consequently renegade 527 entities have become the alternative outlet for deep pockets. An open and aboveboard election process would eliminate the need for such groups and also provide additional sources of funding for candidates without wealth, strengthen our competitive two-party political process, and give all citizens the means to truly exercise their First Amendment rights. It would allow all political factions and candidates to compete equally for the needed funding to exercise their right of free speech.

What would the proposed amendment accomplish?

First, it would strengthen our democracy by restoring political parties to their natural and proper place in our electoral process. Historically, parties have been formed around economic and social issues. They represent to a significant degree the conflicting opinions that prevail in a society at any moment in history. Over the years, our two-party system has satisfied the desire of a vast majority of citizens that their views be sufficiently represented in any ongoing political debate.

Contributions to parties have thus been the primary way for citizens to express their general economic and social views as well as their support for specific candidates. The restriction on large donations has substantially diminished the magnitude and variety of our nation's economic, political, and social dialogue. To suggest that contributions to political parties are somehow corrupting is to misunderstand the very nature of political parties.

Historically, our two major parties have served as a melting pot for the rich, the not-so-rich, and the poor and have acted as a buffer between candidate and contributor, whether it be an individual donor, PAC, or corporation. When parties are functioning naturally, they receive thousands of contributions to a general fund, which they spend selectively on behalf of candidates, issues, get-out-the-votes campaigns, and party functions.

Party committees also make direct contributions to specific candidates. When victorious candidates receive party support, it represents tens of thousands of contributors who have given to the general fund as well as to the respective party leadership. It is to the party that these candidates feel indebted, and they repay that debt by voting with the party in the House or Senate, which saves America from the vexing problem of coalition government.

Thus the proposed amendment would restore the commingling process that the Congress and the Supreme Court have destroyed.

Second, the proposed amendment would release additional funds into an electoral process desperately in need of revitalization. Those who think there is already too much money in politics are simply ignorant of the empirical evidence. The more challengers can spend, the more information voters gain. And the more information voters gain, the more empowered the voters feel and the more competitive congressional elections become.

An election is not just about selecting a winner. It is also about educating citizens on the issues and exposing voters to all the viewpoints surrounding any given issue. Add a million dollars to the campaign of an incumbent congressman and the challenger, and you will see the incumbent's margin of victory narrow and perhaps even disappear. Even if the incumbent spends $2.5 million and the challenger only $1.1 million, instead of $1.5 million and $100,000 respectively, the debate will be fairer and more balanced and the election therefore more genuinely competitive, which would generate much more public interest and participation. Once there is enough money on both sides of a contest, the voters can hear and evaluate each candidate's message, and the supposed corruptive influence of money disappears.

The underlying strength of our election process lies in the competition of ideas, the competition of candidates, and an informed electorate. Take away any one component, and you weaken the system. Weaken or eliminate all three of these elements, as campaign finance reform has done, and you are courting long-term disaster.

The third result of the proposed amendment would be to put an end to the persistent and misguided attempts on the part of several generations of politicians to achieve perfection in a radically imperfect world. Meddling with the system originally devised by the Framers is always risky and usually disastrous. The unintended consequences of a succession of campaign reform laws have proved this point. America survived and prospered for nearly two centuries under the political system set up by the Founders. We should be inclined to think they got it mostly right.

Fourth, the amendment will prevent the trend, already evident, toward a proliferation of parties, along with the inevitable consequence of such a trend: European-style coalition government. Multiparty elections, always regarded as anomalies in the history of American politics, have again emerged in recent decades, as the two major parties have been weakened by a succession of federal laws and court rulings.

Fifth, and perhaps most important of all, the amendment would free the electoral process by returning to the people their right to create political organizations and fund political candidates as they choose. This right predates the establishment of the "more perfect union" and was protected by the preamble to the Constitution and by the First, Ninth, and Tenth Amendments. Freedom, for all its pitfalls and heartaches, is a better arbiter of political conflict than government is. The democratic process devised by the Framers is messy and complicated. But it is still better than any other alternative yet devised.

Passage of the proposed amendment would not be easy, as Article V of the Constitution suggests:

> The Congress, whenever two thirds of both Houses shall deem it necessary, shall propose Amendments to this Constitution, or, on the Application of the Legislatures of two thirds of the several States, shall call a Convention for proposing Amendments, which, in either Case, shall be valid to all Intents and Purposes, as Part of this Constitution, when ratified by the Legislatures of three fourths of the States, or by Conventions in three fourths thereof, as the one or the other Mode of Ratification may be proposed by the Congress; Provided that no Amendment which may be made prior to the Year One thousand eight hundred and eight shall in any Manner affect the first and fourth Clauses in the Ninth Section of the first Article; and that no State, without its Consent, shall be deprived of equal Suffrage in that Senate.

Obviously, the same House and Senate that passed the Bipartisan Campaign Reform Act in 2002 could not be expected to propose a constitutional amendment that would remove Congress's jurisdiction over its own election. Proponents of such an amendment would face two formidable obstacles: (1) the natural reluctance of Congress (or any other government agency) to relinquish any power and (2) the knowledge that freedom would mean greater election competition. This in turn would add pliability to the protective shield of incumbency that has kept so many in office for so long. Yet even with the ratification of the proposed amendment, incumbents would still be hard to defeat. But their margin of victory would be much smaller and our election process would be much stronger.

The hope that two-thirds of both houses would surrender such advantages is vain indeed. If one-third of each body were to vote for the amendment, it would have to be considered a moral victory. Therefore, two-thirds of the legislatures of the states would have to agree to call a constitutional convention for the *sole* purpose of considering this one amendment. This would minimize the risk of utilizing a method of amending that has never yet been tried. Structuring a convention so that it could deal only with the question of restoration of citizen sovereignty would eliminate the possibility that it would attempt to deal with other issues. As the likelihood of such a convention gained strength, it might motivate both Houses of Congress to eliminate the need for such a convention. They could pass the amendment and, with the concurrence of three-quarters of the states, restore to the people the sovereignty that is the foundation of our Constitution.

Immediate change, then, is highly improbable. People must first understand what has been lost over the years and why that loss is important to the survival of our republic. At present, the trend toward greater consolidation of federal power seems all but irreversible.

When the torch of liberty was lit by the Founding Fathers over two hundred years ago, there had been no major democracy on Earth for two thousand years. The Founders based their new democracy on a sacred set of principles with citizen sovereignty as the foundation. At issue today is the extinction of the wick that has enabled that flame of liberty to freely burn for over two centuries. The spark that can save this flame lies in a rediscovery of the principles that are rooted in our heritage and are the core of our Constitution. The Framers vested the power to elect representatives in the people; campaign finance reform has made it impossible for the people to knowledgeably exercise this right. If campaign reform is allowed to stand, voting in America will one day be a ritual with little or no meaning.

EPILOGUE

A final note, especially to the men and women of the press: if the people of America are ever to regain their right of free speech and citizen sovereignty, it will only be because the print and electronic media alert them to the truth of what has happened and urge them to take action. I sincerely hope the press realizes the importance of this challenge because it is not only good for the long-term well being of the country; it is also in the self-interest of the press itself.

America's unique form of democracy was designed to provide a political marketplace where ideas and candidates can freely compete. It is a forum where the people can easily access a broad spectrum of political information from which they can make informed and educated decisions. Political parties are a product of competing interests within this marketplace, and their right and privilege to exchange unrestrained debate during political campaigns is vital to sustaining and protecting our freedom.

A country can have elections and not be a democracy, as in the case of Saddam Hussein's Iraq and the former Soviet Union. But a country cannot be a democracy without open and fair elections. In Iraq, Saddam Hussein received 100 percent of the vote. To emphasize their loyalty some voters even marked their ballots in their own blood. However, most observers would agree that such "elections" did not make Iraq a democracy.

With the imposition of so-called campaign finance reform, our unique form of democracy has been moving toward a stagnating political process in which the voters simply ratify the status quo. With 95 percent or more of the members of the House being regularly reelected and with most members of the Senate only being vulnerable to defeat by opponents with extreme wealth, it should be obvious that our democracy is in trouble. The Supreme Court's declaring all the major provisions of the Bipartisan Campaign Reform Act constitutional has only made things worse. It won't be long now before election to the House is tantamount to an appointment for life and membership in the Senate mostly the prerogative of a wealthy elite. What kind of democracy will our country be when this occurs?

Imposing financial restrictions on political campaigns infringes on the opportunity of nonwealthy citizens to campaign for and win election to office. Campaign finance reforms encourage and aid incumbents and the wealthy to retain political power by imposing financial disadvantages and hardships on lesser-known opponents without wealth. By supporting campaign finance reform, the American people are forfeiting their First Amendment rights in favor of federal regulations that are perpetuating a trend towards rule by a select, privileged few.

This observation, I hope, will be understood as nonpartisan. The present system hurts nonwealthy challengers of all political stripes while favoring whoever is holding the reins of power, whether Republican, Democrat, or independent.

As I have noted, the media play an important role in framing the issue of campaign finance reform. There is a remarkable uniformity in how the media have portrayed the issue and promoted it to the public historically. Typically, media coverage of campaign finance reform is and has been favorable.

And, again, this institutional bias is hardly new. As Sidney Milkis has noted, "There emerged by the late 1870s a national mass press that 'exposed,' even sensationalized, the sins of the new political economy."[1] In response to the Tillman Act in the early 1900s, conscientious journalists, labeled muckrakers, rallied with progressive reformers to urge Congress to "reduce the influence of money in politics."[2]

The press's view of the Federal Election Campaign Acts and *Buckley v. Valeo* decision in the 1970s also was favorable. In fact, the principal criticism was that the media were not active enough in reporting the "scandals" of undisclosed campaign contributions.[3] With the turn of the twenty-first century, the national press continued to be primarily advocates of campaign finance reform legislation.

Herein lies the ultimate irony: the very institution that has always defended free speech (the press) has abandoned it at its most crucial hour. In the very process in which free speech is most important—electing our public officials—the media fails to frame campaign finance reform in terms of constitutionally guaranteed freedom of speech. Instead, they rail on about fairness and the "little guy" against the "big corporations."

How the media could abandon the First Amendment in making such arguments is befuddling at best, corrupt at worst, given that the media are conveniently exempt from the campaign finance reform laws most of them so eagerly advocate. The media shamelessly perpetuate the myths that money is inherently evil and that every citizen's right to free speech must be given up in exchange for more federal government regulations or else money will destroy the integrity of the entire political process.

Sadly, public opinion has largely mirrored the media's assumption that money will always be a corrupting influence in politics. Since public opinion polling began decades ago, nearly two-thirds of people have thought new campaign finance laws were a good idea and supported spending limits in campaigns. Most people consistently fail to make the connection between campaign finance reform and the loss of freedom of expression and citizen sovereignty.

The truth is that, under the guise of reform, we often make matters worse. The reason Americans are seduced by reform is that it appeals to our national optimism. If something's wrong, we Americans think we can fix it. We are a nation of compulsive problem-solvers. Unfortunately the word *reform* has become a public-relations tool. It has become a convenient label that can be slapped on any proposal in order to claim the moral high ground. Too often reform is used as a packaging device: reform is good; all opponents of reform are bad. When the press repeatedly frames the issue of campaign finance in terms of "reform," it shifts the argument away from substance and toward symbolism. This tactic suppresses serious debate.

In these pages I hope I have presented some evidence that will help foster a legitimate debate based on principles and practicality. I hope the national media, after examining the data provided here, come to the same conclusion I have, namely that campaign finance reform has had a devastating effect on the fairness and health of federal elections. When a party and its candidates need lawyers to determine what they can and cannot do, we have entered an era of constitutional censorship. The media need to alert the citizenry about what is really happening so they can begin to understand what they are losing. Only then will the people take the steps necessary to reclaim their sovereignty and First Amendment rights.

It is important to challenge historical assumptions that campaign finance reform is a good thing and to frame a national discussion on the subject that is based on concrete evidence and accurate information about the history of campaign finance reform in the United States, a dialogue about campaign finance reform based on data and actual outcomes, not slogans, finger-pointing, and posturing.

I believe that conservatives and liberals, Democrats and Republicans, and the many disaffected independents can work together toward real reforms that will improve our system and further democracy rather than undermining it. As Americans, we have it within our power to keep ourselves free. Unalienable rights cannot be taken away. They can only be surrendered.

NOTES

Chapter 1. The Folly of Reform

1. Most of the major provisions of the 1974 FECA regarding contribution limits were declared constitutional by the Supreme Court in its controversial *Buckley v. Valeo* decision rendered in January 1976.

2. The Bipartisan Campaign Reform Act of 2002 is also referred to as McCain-Feingold after its cosponsors in the United States Senate. In December 2003, the Supreme Court, in another highly controversial decision, declared all the major provisions of the act constitutional in its *McConnell v. Federal Election Commission* decision.

3. Seven in ten support new campaign finance legislation. J. M. Jones, *Gallup Poll Monthly* 437 (February 2002): 32–33.

4. The statistical information for the post-Buckley era covers only the period 1976–2000. At the time of computation, the 2001–2002 data were not available.

5. Given that the eleven former Confederate states emerged from the Civil War as a rock-solid single-party region and remained so until the latter part of the twentieth century, these states have been excluded from the Senate data in Tables 1.3 and 1.4.

Chapter 2. The Rise and Fall of Citizen Sovereignty

1. Jones, *Gallup Poll Monthly* 437, 32–33.

2. D. M. Moore, "Widespread Public Support for Campaign Finance Reform," *Gallup Poll Monthly* 426 (March 2001): 41–42.

3. George H. Gallup, *The Gallup Poll: Public Opinion, 1935–1971* (New York, 1972), 1:136, 401.

4. Ibid., 3:2070, 2129, 2272.

Chapter 3. Rome: A Flawed Model

1. Thomas Jefferson, "Query 13," *Notes on the State of Virginia* (1787; Chapel Hill, 1954), 121–26.

2. *Rome: Power and Glory,* VHS. (Questar, 2001). For a recent in-depth history and analysis of the Roman constitution, see Andrew Lintott, *The Constitution of the Roman Republic* (New York, 1999).

Chapter 4. Citizen Sovereignty: The Dearest Thing of All

1. James I, "Address to Dissolve Parliament" (1610).
2. John Locke, *The Second Treatise of Government* (1690; New York, 2004), 14.
3. Alexis de Tocqueville, *Democracy in America,* trans. Henry Reeve (1835; New York, 2000), 61.
4. Ibid, 62.

Chapter 5. The Constitution and America's First Political Campaign

1. Patrick Henry, speech before the Virginia ratifying convention, June 5, 1789, in *The Complete Anti-Federalist,* 7 vols., ed. Herbert J. Storing and Murry Dry (Chicago, 1981), 5:22.
2. James Madison, Federalist No. 10, "The Same Subject Continued: The Union as a Safeguard against Domestic Faction and Insurrection," in Alexander Hamilton, James Madison, and John Jay, *The Federalist Papers* (1788; New York, 1982), 50–58.
3. Ibid., 51.
4. Ibid.
5. Ibid., 51–52.
6. Ibid.

Chapter 7. What Is an Election, Anyway?

1. Thomas Jefferson, First Inaugural Address, in *The Writings of Thomas Jefferson,* Memorial Edition (Washington, DC, 1903–4), 3:31.
2. Thomas Jefferson, quoted in Saul K. Padover, *Jefferson: A Great American's Life and Ideas* (New York, 1952), 89.

Chapter 9. The Perceived Corruption of Money versus the Real Corruption of Power

1. "Virginia Resolution: 1798," posted at www.yale.edu/lawweb/avalon/virres.htm by the Avalon Project at Yale Law School.
2. Thomas Jefferson to Joseph Priestly, March 21, 1801, in *Writings of Thomas Jefferson,* 10:229.
3. *McConnell v. Federal Election Commission,* 540 U.S. 93 (2003), 40.
4. Dimitri B. Papadimitriou, preface to *Campaign Contributions, Policy Decisions, and Election Outcomes: A Study of the Effects of Campaign Finance Reform,* by Christopher Magee, Jerome Levy Economics Institute of Bard College Public Policy Brief no. 64 (Blithewood, Annandale-on-Hudson, NY, 2001), 5.
5. Bradley A. Smith, *Unfree Speech: The Folly of Campaign Finance Reform* (Princeton, NJ, 2003), 135.
6. Stephen Ansolabehere, John M. de Figueiredo, and James M. Snyder, "Are Campaign Contributions Investment in the Political Marketplace or Individual Consumption? Or 'Why Is There So Little Money in Politics?'" MIT Sloan School of Management Working Paper no. 4272-02 (October 2002), 19 (quote), 9–13.
7. *Buckley v. Valeo,* 424 U.S. 1 (1976), quoting *Roth v. United States,* 354 U.S. 476, 484 (1957).
8. Ibid.

9. Ibid.

10. Edward J. Erler, "Was Madison Wrong? Is Campaign Finance Reform Right?" *Imprimis* 31, no. 4 (April 2002), 3.

11. *Buckley v. Valeo,* 424 U.S. 1 (1976).

12. James Madison, Federalist No. 51, "The Structure of the Government Must Furnish the Proper Checks and Balances between the Different Departments," in Hamilton, Madison, and Jay, *Federalist Papers,* 316.

13. Benjamin Franklin, speech before the Constitutional Convention, Sept. 17, 1787, quoted in *The Debates in the Federal Convention of 1787,* ed. Gaillard Hunt and James Brown Scott (New York, 1920), accessed at the Avalon Project at Yale Law School, http://elsinore.cis.yale.edu/lawweb/avalon/debates/917.htm.

14. *Gibbons v. Ogden,* 22 U.S. 1 (1824).

15. *Marbury v. Madison,* 5 U.S. 137 (1803).

16. Charles Evans Hughes, *The Autobiographical Notes of Charles Evans Hughes,* ed. David J. Danelski and Joseph S. Tulchin (Cambridge, MA, 1973), 144.

17. David M. Primo, *Public Opinion and Campaign Finance: A Skeptical Look at Senator McCain's Claims,* CATO Institute Briefing Paper 60 (Washington, DC, 2001), 5.

18. Alexander Hamilton, Federalist No. 78, "The Judiciary Department," in Hamilton, Madison, and Jay, *Federalist Papers,* 472.

Chapter 10. We the Sovereigns, Not We the Subjects

1. Theodore Roosevelt to George Cortelyou, October 26, 1904, *The Works of Theodore Roosevelt,* Memorial Edition, ed. Hermann Hagedorn (New York, 1923–26), 23:379–80.

2. *Tillman Act of 1907* (18 USC 610).

Chapter 11. The Crux of the Problem

1. Michael J. Malbin, *Life after Reform: When the Bipartisan Campaign Reform Act Meets Politics,* ed. Michael J. Malbin (Lanham, MD, 2003), 22.

2. George Orwell, *Animal Farm: A Fairy Story,* Centennial Edition (New York, 2003), 92.

3. Anatole France, quoted in John Bartlett, *Familiar Quotations,* ed. Emily Morison Beck (Boston, 1980), 655.

4. Elizabeth Drew, *The Corruption of American Politics: What Went Wrong and Why* (Woodstock, NY, 1999), 2.

5. James Madison, Federalist 51, 316.

Chapter 12. Supreme Court Mandates Run Amok

1. Thomas Jefferson, quoted in Deborah O'Toole, "Political Parties," article for electronic journal *Ambermont Magazine,* http://deborahotoole.tripod.com/Political/.

2. Jeanne Cummings, "Those 527 Fund-Raisers Prove Resilient; Republicans, Slow off the Blocks, Now May Act to Get Rid of Them," *Wall Street Journal,* December 6, 2004.

3. Center for Voting and Democracy, press release, July 2, 2002.

4. *Marbury v. Madison,* 5 U.S. 37 (1803).

Chapter 13. Empirical Evidence

1. *Buckley v. Valeo,* 424 U.S. 1 (1976).

2. Center for Responsive Politics, "Gender Gap, GOP Edge in Small Donations Could Loom Big in 2004 Elections," June 27, 2003, www.opensecrets.org/pressreleases/DonorDemog.asp.

3. R. T. Barton, "The First Election of Washington to the House of Burgesses," New River Notes, www.ls.net/~newriver/va/1electgw.htm.

4. A conservative estimate obtained using the inflation calculator developed by S. Morgan Friedman at www.westegg.com/inflation/. A similar form at www.austintxgensoc.org/calculate cpi.html yields an estimate more than twice this amount, $5.40.

Chapter 14. Freedom of the Press

1. Willmoore Kendall and George W. Carey, *The Basic Symbols of the American Political Tradition* (Baton Rouge, LA, 1970), 30–42.

Chapter 15. Political Fund-Raising: The Current Reality

1. U.S. Census Bureau, Resident Population plus Armed Forces Overseas—Estimates by Age, Sex, and Race: July 1, 1976, www.census.gov/popest/archives/pre-1980/PE-11-1976.pdf.

2. U.S. Census Bureau, Table DP-1, Profile of General Demographic Characteristics: 2000, http://factfinder.census.gov.

3. Geoffrey E. Meredith and Charles D. Schewe, *Defining Markets, Defining Moments: America's 7 Generational Cohorts, Their Shared Experiences, and Why Businesses Should Care* (New York, 2002).

4. Federal Election Commission news release, "PAC Activity Increases for 2002 Elections," March 27, 2003, www.fec.gov/press/press2003/20030327pac/20030327pac.html.

Chapter 16. The Twenty-eighth Ammendment

1. "Top 100 Daily Newspapers in the United States," from *Editor and Publisher International Yearbook* (2003), www.infoplease.com/ipea/A0004420.html.

2. Pete du Pont, "Doubting Thomas: Incumbents Throw Jefferson's Principles Overboard and Scurry for the Lifeboats," *Wall Street Journal,* March 28, 2001; "A Self-Serving Senate: McCain-Feingold Is an Incumbent-Protection Racket," *Wall Street Journal,* March 25, 2001; "Campaign Fairy Tale: This Kind of Reform Doesn't Deserve Respect," *Wall Street Journal,* March 29, 2001.

3. Jonathon Chait, "Reformulation," *New Republic,* September 8–15, 1997, 15–16.

4. Steve Largent, letter to fellow House members, June 21, 2001.

5. Smith, *Unfree Speech,* 81.

6. Bruce Buchanan, *Presidential Campaign Quality: Incentives and Reform* (Upper Saddle River, NJ, 2004), 10.

7. Josh Gerstein, *ABC News,* April 27, 2001, www.abcnews.go.com (accessed June 3, 2004).

8. See Campaign Finance Special Report, a selection of recent opinion pieces and editorials from the *Washington Post,* http://washingtonpost.com/wp-srv/politics/special/campfin/opinion.htm; David S. Broder, "Campaign Reformers at War," *Washington Post,* May 20, 1998.

9. Gerstein, *ABC News,* April 27, 2001.

10. "Perils for Campaign Reform," editorial, *New York Times,* March 27, 2001, quoted by Gerstein.

Epilogue

1. Sidney M. Milkis, "Theodore Roosevelt and the Birth of the Modern Presidency," *Miller Center Report* 19, no. 3 (Fall/Winter 2003): 25.

2. Anthony Corrado, "Money and Politics: A History of Federal Campaign Finance Law," in Corrado et al., *The New Campaign Finance Sourcebook* (forthcoming), http://www.brookings .edu/gs/cf/newsourcebk.htm, 6.

3. Herbert E. Alexander and Brian A Haggerty, eds., *The Federal Election Campaign Act: After a Decade of Political Reform* (Los Angeles, 1981), 17, 42.

BIBLIOGRAPHY

Abraham, Henry J. *The Judiciary: The Supreme Court in the Governmental Process*. 8th ed. Dubuque, IA, 1991.

Ackerman, Bruce. *Reconstructing American Law*. Cambridge, MA, 1984.

Alexander, Herbert E., and Brian A. Haggerty, eds. *The Federal Election Campaign Act: After a Decade of Political Reform*. Report of a conference sponsored by Citizens' Research Foundation, University of California, Washington, DC, April 2–3, 1981. Los Angeles, 1981.

Allen, Steven W. *Founding Fathers: Uncommon Heroes*. Mesa, AZ, 2002.

Anderson, Thornton. *Creating the Constitution: The Convention of 1787 and the First Congress*. University Park, PA, 1993.

Ansolabehere, Stephen, John M. P. de Figueiredo, and James M. Snyder. "Are Campaign Contributions Investment in the Political Marketplace or Individual Consumption? Or 'Why Is There So Little Money in Politics?'" MIT Sloan School of Management Working Paper no. 4272-02 (October 2002).

Ashworth, Marjorie. *To Create a Nation: The Constitutional Convention of 1787*. McLean, VA, 1987.

Bailyn, Bernard. *The Ideological Origins of the American Revolution*. Cambridge, MA, 1967.

Baum, Lawrence. *American Courts: Process and Policy*. 3rd ed. Boston, 1994.

Becker, Carl L. *The Declaration of Independence: A Study in the History of Political Ideas*. New York, 1942.

Benton, Wilbourn E., ed. *1787: Drafting the U.S. Constitution*. College Station, TX, 1986.

Berger, Raoul. *Government by Judiciary: The Transformation of the Fourteenth Amendment*. Cambridge, MA, 1977.

Bickel, Alexander. *The Least Dangerous Branch: The Supreme Court at the Bar of Politics*. Indianapolis, 1962.

———. *The Supreme Court and the Idea of Progress*. New York, 1970.

Bishop, Joseph Bucklin. *Theodore Roosevelt and His Time Shown in His Own Letters*. 2 vols. New York, 1920.

Bork, Robert. *The Tempting of America: The Political Seduction of the Law*. New York, 1990.

Bowen, Catherine Drinker. *Miracle at Philadelphia: The Story of the Constitutional Convention, May to September, 1787.* Boston, 1966.

Bradford, M. E. *A Better Guide Than Reason: Studies in the American Revolution.* La Salle, IL, 1979.

———. *Founding Fathers: Brief Lives of the Framers.* Lawrence, KS, 1994.

———. *Original Intentions: On the Making and Ratification of the United States Constitution.* Athens, GA, 1993.

Brant, Irving. *The Bill of Rights: Its Origin and Meaning.* Indianapolis, 1965.

———. *James Madison.* 6 vols. Indianapolis, 1941–61.

Buchanan, Bruce. *Presidential Campaign Quality: Incentives and Reform.* Upper Saddle River, NJ, 2004.

Buckley v. Valeo. 424 U.S. 1 (1976).

Burke, Edmund. *Empire and Community: Edmund Burke's Writings and Speeches on International Relations.* Ed. David P. Fiddler and Jennifer M. Welsh. Boulder, CO, 1999.

Burnett, Edmund Cody. *The Continental Congress.* Westport, CT, 1975.

Burns, James MacGregor. *The Deadlock of Democracy: Four-Party Politics in America.* Englewood Cliffs, NJ, 1963.

Burroughs v. United States. 290 U.S. 534, 545 (1934).

Cardozo, Benjamin N. *The Growth of the Law.* New Haven, CT, 1934.

———. *The Nature of the Judicial Process.* New Haven, CT, 1921.

———. *The Paradoxes of Legal Science.* New York, 1928.

Carmichael, Orton H. *Lincoln's Gettysburg Address.* New York, 1917.

Caro, Robert A. *The Years of Lyndon Johnson: Master of the Senate.* New York, 2002.

Jonathon Chait, "Reformulation." *New Republic,* September 8–15, 1997, 15–16.

Churchill, Winston S. *A History of the English-Speaking Peoples.* 4 vols. New York, 1956–58.

Collier, Christopher, and James Lincoln Collier. *Decision in Philadelphia: The Constitutional Convention of 1787.* New York, 1986.

Corrado, Anthony, et al. *Campaign Finance Reform: A Sourcebook.* Washington, DC, 1997.

———. *Inside the Campaign Finance Battle: Court Testimony on the New Reforms.* Washington, DC, 2003.

———. "Money and Politics: A History of Federal Campaign Finance Law." In Anthony Corrado et al., *The New Campaign Finance Sourcebook* (forthcoming), www.brookings.edu/gs/cf/newsourcebk.htm.

Corwin, Edward S. *Constitutional Revolution, Ltd.* Claremont, CA, 1946.

———. *The "Higher Law" Background of American Constitutional Law.* Ithaca, NY, 1955.

Cox, Archibald. *The Court and the Constitution.* Boston, 1987.

Croly, Herbert. *The Promise of American Life.* New York, 1911.

Jeanne Cummings, "Those 527 Fund-Raisers Prove Resilient; Republicans, Slow off the Blocks, Now May Act to Get Rid of Them," *Wall Street Journal,* December 6, 2004.

Dahl, Robert. *Democracy and Its Critics.* New Haven, CT, 1989.

DeRosa, Marshall L. *The Confederate Constitution of 1861: An Inquiry into American Constitutionalism.* Columbia, MO, 1991.

———. *The Ninth Amendment and the Politics of Creative Jurisprudence: Disparaging the Fundamental Right of Popular Control.* New Brunswick, NJ, 1996.

Drew, Elizabeth. *The Corruption of American Politics: What Went Wrong and Why.* Woodstock, NY, 1999.

Dye, Thomas R. *American Federalism: Competition among Governments.* Lexington, MA, 1990.

Elkin, Stephen L. and Soltan, Karol Edward. *A New Constitutionalism: Designing Political Institutions for a Good Society.* Chicago, 1993.

Elliot, Jonathan, ed. *The Debates in the Several State Conventions on the Adoption of the Federal Constitution, as Recommended by the General Convention at Philadelphia, in 1787.* 5 vols. 1836–45. Buffalo, 1996.

Ellis, Joseph J. *Founding Brothers: The Revolutionary Generation.* New York, 2000.

Ely, James W. *The Guardian of Every Other Right: A Constitutional History of Property Rights.* New York, 1992.

Ely, John Hart. *Democracy and Distrust: A Theory of Judicial Review.* Cambridge, MA, 1980.

Erler, Edward J. "Was Madison Wrong? Is Campaign Finance Reform Right?" *Imprimis* 31, no. 4 (April 2002): 4–7.

Ettenberg, Elliott. *The Next Economy: Will You Know Where Your Customers Are?* New York, 2002.

Evans, M. Stanton. *The Theme Is Freedom: Religion, Politics, and the American Tradition.* Washington, DC, 1994.

Falk, Ericka. "Issue Advocacy Advertising through the Presidential Primary 1999–2000 Election Cycle." Philadelphia, 2000.

Farrand, Max, ed. *The Records of the Federal Convention of 1787.* New Haven, CT, 1911.

Fishkin, James S. *The Dialogue of Justice: Toward a Self-Reflective Society.* New Haven, CT, 1992.

Fitzpatrick, John C. *The Spirit of Revolution: New Light from Some of the Original Sources of American History.* New York, 1924.

Frank, Jerome. *Law and the Modern Mind.* Garden City, NY, 1930.

Franklin, Benjamin. "Silence Dogood, No. 8." *New-England Courant,* July 9, 1722.

———. *Vermont Declaration of Rights,* Article 18. 1793.

Friedenwald, Herbert. *The Declaration of Independence: An Interpretation and an Analysis.* New York, 1974.

Gallup, George H. *The Gallup Poll: Public Opinion, 1935–1971.* 3 vols. New York, 1972.

Gibbons v. Ogden. 22 U.S. 1 (1824).

Goodwin, Jason. *Greenback: The Almighty Dollar and the Invention of America.* New York, 2003.

Hall, Arnold Bennett. *Popular Government: An Inquiry into the Nature and Methods of Representative Government.* New York, 1921.

Hamilton, Alexander, James Madison, and John Jay. *The Federalist Papers.* 1788. New York, 1982.

Hazelton, John H. *The Declaration of Independence: Its History.* New York, 1970.

Henderson, H. James. *Party Politics in the Continental Congress.* Lanham, MD, 1987.

Hill, Steven. *Fixing Elections: The Failure of America's Winner-Take-All Politics.* New York, 2002.

Himmelfarb, Gertrude. *Lord Acton: A Study in Conscience and Politics.* Chicago, 1952.

Holland, Tom. *Rubicon: The Last Years of the Roman Republic.* New York, 2003.

Hughes, Charles Evans. *The Autobiographical Notes of Charles Evans Hughes.* Ed. David J. Danelski and Joseph S. Tulchin. Cambridge, MA, 1973.

Hunt, Gaillard, and James Brown Scott, eds. *The Debates in the Federal Convention of 1787.* New York, 1920.

Hutson, James H., ed. *Supplement to Max Farrand's "The Records of the Federal Convention of 1787."* New Haven, CT, 1987.

Jaffa, Harry. *How to Think about the American Revolution.* Durham, NC, 1978.

James I. "Address to Dissolve Parliament." 1610.

Jefferson, Thomas. *The Best Letters of Thomas Jefferson.* Ed. J. G. de Roulhac Hamilton. Boston, 1926.

———. *Notes on the State of Virginia.* 1787. Chapel Hill, 1954.

———. *The Writings of Thomas Jefferson.* Memorial Edition. 20 vols. Ed. Albert A. Lipscomb and Albert Ellery Bergh. Washington, DC, 1903–4.

Jensen, Merrill. *The Articles of Confederation: An Interpretation of the Social-Constitutional History of the American Revolution.* Madison, WI, 1940.

———, ed. *The Documentary History of the Ratification of the Constitution.* Madison, WI, 1976.

Jillson, Calvin, and Rick K. Wilson. *Congressional Dynamics: Structure, Coordination, and Choice in the First American Congress, 1774–1789.* Stanford, CA, 1994.

Johnson, Paul. *A History of the American People.* New York, 1998.

Jones, J. M. *Gallup Poll Monthly* 437 (February 2002): 32–33.

Kammen, Michael. *A Machine That Would Go of Itself: The Constitution in American Culture.* New York, 1987.

Kelly, Alfred Hinsey, Winifred A. Harbison, and Herman Belz. *The American Constitution: Its Origins and Development.* 6th ed. New York, 1983.

Kendall, Willmoore, and George W. Carey. *The Basic Symbols of the American Political Tradition.* Baton Rouge, LA, 1970.

Ketcham, Ralph. *James Madison: A Biography.* New York, 1971.

Koch, Adrienne. *Jefferson and Madison: The Great Collaboration.* New York, 1950.

Krabbe, Hugo. *The Modern Idea of the State.* New York, 1922.

Lambakis, Steven James. *Winston Churchill, Architect of Peace: A Study of Statesmanship and the Cold War.* Westport, CT, 1993.

Lasser, William. *The Limits of Judicial Power: The Supreme Court in American Politics.* Chapel Hill, NC, 1988.

Levy, Leonard W., and Dennis J. Mahoney, eds. *The Framing and Ratification of the Constitution.* New York, 1987.

Liberty: The American Revolution. VHS. Twin Cities Public Television, 1997.

Library of Congress. Legislative Reference Service. *Documents Illustrative of the Formation of the Union of the American States.* Selected, arranged, and indexed by Charles C. Tansill. Washington, DC, 1927.

Lintott, Andrew. *The Constitution of the Roman Republic.* New York, 1999.

Locke, John. *The Second Treatise of Government.* 1690. New York, 2004.

Lutz, Donald S. *The Origins of American Constitutionalism.* Baton Rouge, LA, 1988.

———. *A Preface to American Political Theory.* Lawrence, KS, 1992.

Madison, James. "Virginia Resolution of 1798." http://www.constitution.org/cons/virg1798.htm.

Magee, Christopher. *Campaign Contributions, Policy Decisions and Election Outcomes: A Study of the Effects of Campaign Finance Reform.* Jerome Levy Economics Institute of Bard College Public Policy Brief no. 64. Blithewood, Annandale-on-Hudson, NY, 2001.

Malbin, Michael J., ed. *Life after Reform: When the Bipartisan Campaign Finance Reform Act Meets Politics.* Lanham, MD, 2003.

Malone, Dumas. *The Story of the Declaration of Independence.* New York, 1975.

Maltz, Earl M. *Rethinking Constitutional Law: Originalism, Interventionism, and the Politics of Judicial Review.* Lawrence, KS, 1994.

Marbury v. Madison, 5 U.S. 137 (1803).

Matthews, Richard K. *If Men Were Angels: James Madison and the Heartless Empire of Reason.* Lawrence, KS, 1995.

McCloskey, Robert G. *The American Supreme Court.* Chicago, 1960.

McConnell v. Federal Election Commission. 540 U.S. 93 (2003).

McCoy, Drew R. *The Elusive Republic: Political Economy in Jeffersonian America.* Chapel Hill, NC, 1980.

McDonald, Forrest. *Novus Ordo Seclorum: The Intellectual Origins of the Constitution.* Lawrence, KS, 1985.

———. *We the People: The Economic Origins of the Constitution.* Chicago, 1958.

McDowell, Gary L. *Curbing the Courts: The Constitution and the Limits of Judicial Power.* Baton Rouge, LA, 1988.

McLaughlin, Andrew C. *The Foundations of American Constitutionalism.* New York, 1932.

McNeilly, Mark. *Sun Tzu and the Art of Modern Warfare*. New York, 2001.

Meredith, Geoffrey E., and Charles D. Schewe. *Defining Markets, Defining Moments: America's 7 Generational Cohorts, Their Shared Experiences, and Why Businesses Should Care*. New York, 2002.

Milkis, Sidney M. "Theodore Roosevelt and the Birth of the Modern Presidency." *Miller Center Report* 19, no. 3 (Fall/Winter 2003): 22–27.

Miller, James C., III. *Monopoly Politics*. Stanford, CA, 1999.

Monroe, James. *The Political Writings of James Monroe*. Ed. James P. Lucier. Washington, DC, 2001.

Montross, Lynn. *The Reluctant Rebels: The Story of the Continental Congress, 1774–1789*. New York, 1970.

Moore, D. M. "Widespread Public Support for Campaign Finance Reform." *Gallup Poll Monthly* 426 (March 2001): 41–42.

Morris, Edmund. *Theodore Rex*. New York, 2001.

Morris, Richard B. *Seven Who Shaped Our Destiny: The Founding Fathers as Revolutionaries*. New York, 1973.

Neely, Richard. *How Courts Govern America*. New Haven, CT, 1981.

Onuf, Peter S., ed. *Congress and the Confederation*. New York, 1991.

Orwell, George. *Animal Farm: A Fairy Story*. 1945. Centennial Edition. New York, 2003.

Padover, Saul K. *Jefferson: A Great American's Life and Ideas*. New York, 1952.

Peppers, Don, and Martha Rogers. *Enterprise One to One: Tools for Competing in the Interactive Age*. New York, 1997.

———. *The One to One Future: Building Relationships One Customer at a Time*. New York, 1993.

Perkins, Dexter. *Charles Evans Hughes and American Democratic Statesmanship*. Boston, 1956.

Phelps, Glenn A. *George Washington and American Constitutionalism*. Lawrence, KS, 1993.

Pound, Roscoe. *Law Finding through Experience and Reason: Three Lectures*. Athens, GA, 1960.

———. *Social Control through Law*. New Haven, CT, 1942.

Primo, David M. *Public Opinion and Campaign Finance: A Skeptical Look at Senator McCain's Claims*. CATO Institute Briefing Paper 60 (Washington, DC, 2001).

Rakove, Jack N. *The Beginnings of National Politics: An Interpretive History of the Continental Congress*. Baltimore, MD, 1982.

Rasor, Eugene L. *General Douglas MacArthur, 1880–1964: Historiography and Annotated Bibliography*. Westport, CT, 1994.

Rome: Power and Glory. VHS. Questar, 2001.

Roosevelt, Theodore. *The Works of Theodore Roosevelt*. Memorial Edition. 24 vols. Ed. Hermann Hagedorn. New York, 1923–26.

Rossiter, Clinton. *1787: The Grand Convention*. New York, 1966.

Rothbard, Murray N. *A History of Money and Banking in the United States: The Colonial Era to World War II*. Auburn, AL, 2002.

Rutland, Robert A., ed. *James Madison and the American Nation, 1751–1836: An Encyclopedia*. New York, 1994.

Schachner, Nathan. *Thomas Jefferson: A Biography*. 1951. New York, 1957.

Scott, James Brown. *James Madison's Notes of Debate in the Federal Convention of 1787 and Their Relation to a More Perfect Society of Nations*. 1918. Union, NJ, 2001.

Simon, Yves R. *The Tradition of Natural Law: A Philosopher's Reflection*. New York, 1965.

Smith, Adam. *An Inquiry into the Nature and Causes of the Wealth of Nations*. 1776. Buffalo, 1991.

Smith, Bradley A. *Unfree Speech: The Folly of Campaign Finance Reform*. Princeton, NJ, 2001.

Smith, James Morton, ed. *The Republic of Letters: The Correspondence between Thomas Jefferson and James Madison, 1776–1826*. New York, 1995.

Smith, Paul H., et al., eds. *Letters of Delegates to Congress, 1774–1789*. 26 vols. Washington, DC, 1976–2000.

Solberg, Winton U., ed. *The Constitutional Convention and the Formation of the Union*. 2nd ed. Urbana, IL, 1990.

Storing, Herbert J., and Murry Dry, eds. *The Complete Anti-Federalist*. 7 vols. Chicago, 1981.

Story, Joseph. *Commentaries on the Constitution of the United States, with a Preliminary Review of the Constitutional History of the Colonies and States before the Adoption of the Constitution*. 3 vols. New York, 1970.

Thurber, James A., and Candice J. Nelson, eds. *Campaign Warriors: The Role of Political Consultants in Elections*. Washington, DC, 2000.

Tocqueville, Alexis de. *Democracy in America*. 1835. New York, 2000.

Tourtoulon, Pierre de. *Philosophy in the Development of Law*. New York, 1922.

Tribe, Laurence H., and Michael C. Dorf. *On Reading the Constitution*. Cambridge, MA, 1991.

Walker, Graham. *Moral Foundations of Constitutional Thought: Current Problems, Augustinian Prospects*. Princeton, NJ, 1990.

Warren, Charles. *The Supreme Court in United States History*. 2 vols. Boston, 1926.

Wigdor, David. *Roscoe Pound: Philosopher of Law*. Westport, CT, 1974.

Wildavsky, Aaron. *The Rise of Radical Egalitarianism*. Washington, DC, 1991.

Williams, Jonathan. *Money: A History*. New York, 1997.

Wills, Garry. *Inventing America: Jefferson's Declaration of Independence*. New York, 1979.

———. *Lincoln at Gettysburg: The Words That Remade America*. New York, 1992.

Winthrop, Robert C. *Washington, Bowdoin, and Franklin, as Portrayed in Occasional Addresses*. Boston, 1876.

Wood, Gordon S. *The Creation of the American Republic, 1776–1787*. Chapel Hill, NC, 1969.

————. *The Making of the Constitution*. Waco, TX, 1987.

Wright, Benjamin Fletcher. *American Interpretations of Natural Law: A Study in the History of Political Thought*. New York, 1962.

Wright, Charles Alan. *The Law of Federal Courts*. 4th ed. St. Paul, MN, 1983.